Francis Reginald Statham

Poems and Sonnets

Francis Reginald Statham

Poems and Sonnets

ISBN/EAN: 9783744712187

Printed in Europe, USA, Canada, Australia, Japan

Cover: Foto ©Thomas Meinert / pixelio.de

More available books at **www.hansebooks.com**

POEMS AND SONNETS

BY
F. REGINALD STATHAM

AUTHOR OF
"GLAPHYRA AND OTHER POEMS," "EUCHARIS: A POEM," &C., &C.

TO MY FRIEND,

FRANCIS WILLIAM REITZ,

PRESIDENT OF THE ORANGE FREE STATE,

THIS VOLUME IS INSCRIBED AS A SMALL

TOKEN OF APPRECIATION AND

REGARD.

CONTENTS.

	PAGE
Gianetta	1
The Beacon	21
Two Rivers	29
A Bridal Song	33
A Southern Christmas	37
Outspanned	42
A Song of Peace	46
Carmen Solare	49
Moloch	52
Grief's Fountain	55
Watching	56
Declining Day	57
A Dagger	58
Ben Ledi	59
A Diamond	60
Why Seek ye the Living?	61
A Serenade	62
A Change of Wind	64
The Vestal	65
Hope in Parting	66

CONTENTS.

	PAGE
The Astronomer	67
A Photograph	68
Thawing	69
Death or Life	70
Conclusions	71
Accepted Love	73
The Stepmother	74
Silent Change	75
"I Shall be Satisfied"	76
Sorrow	77
A Birthday	78
One Blossom	79
A Conjunction	80
Widening Life	82
The Moorland	83
A Wakeful Night	86
The Spring	87
Election	89
"Grant us thy Peace"	90
A Journey	91
Rus in Urbe	92
Hope	93
Maxwell Square	94
Highdown, Freshwater	96
Remembrance	97
Independence	98
By the Esk	99
"Blessed are the Peacemakers"	101
Godspeed	102

CONTENTS.

Whitsuntide	103
Vox Populi	104
Youth in Age	106
Vox Dei	107
Winter in the South	108
The Madonna	109
Patient Work	112
Only	113
Mutual Help	115
The Last Hope	116
Silent Influence	117
"We Might"	118
The Magdalen	120
Evening	121
Holy Ground	122
Parted	124
The Last Martyr	125
Which?	126
Adoption	128
Twilight	129
Forecasting	130
A Song of Solway	131
Help	133
The Violin Player	134
Early Visions	135
A Statue	136
Protection	138
A Dialogue	139
History	141

CONTENTS.

	PAGE
An Anniversary	142
Love and Sorrow	144
Love's Temple	145
Poetry	147
An Oracle	148
A Holiday	149
Prothalamium	150
Judge Not	152
Inconstancy	153
A Revelation	154
Livingstone	155
Responsibility	158
Dirge	159
Growing Old	161
Verbum Sap.	162
Uphill	163
The Poet Speaks	164
Failure	166
First Loss	167
"This Man Calleth for Elias"	168
Quite Happy	169
Partnership	171
Reminiscences	172
Reward in Due Season	173
Old Bogie	174
Association	177
Fairyland	178
Procrastination	180
Child-Dreams	181

CONTENTS.

	PAGE
Self-Knowledge	183
The Ground Swell	184
Compromise	186
Forwards!	187
Work	189
Stewart's Sword	190
On the Threshold	192
The Shadow of Love	193
A Dip into Keats	196
Night and Death	197
Coming Change	198
A Christmas Greeting	199
Light in Darkness	201
The Hope that is in us	202
A. C. Swinburne	204
The Last Waltz	205
"Nihil feci ; amavi tantúm"	207
The Violin's Story	208
In Soundings	210
A Kiss for the Dealer	211
The Lizard Lights	213
A Railway Note	214
A Strand Study	215
In Arcadia	216
Ecce Homo!	218
Her Progress	219
A Question	222
Experience	223
Notes	224

GIANETTA.

"Thrice hast thou met me in the secret hour,
  Calling my name, and yet thyself unknown;
Thrice hath the dayspring's love-disturbing power
  Crept through the night, and found us all alone;
And many times (thyself canst count them best)
Upon thy lips my passion hath been pressed.

"Yet dost thou, like some deity of old,
  Whose form was wrapped in bright celestial mist,
Still shroud thyself; mine eyes may scarce behold
  Even the lips which I so oft have kissed.
Conceal thyself no longer; let me see
At last the face of my divinity."

As rush the tides when Autumn winds are high,
  So rushed the crimson to her listening brow;
As they retire and leave the sands all dry,
  So fled that blush, and left her cheek like snow;
Then love cast out the fear that held her dumb,—
"I will not doubt," she said; "the time is come."

One backward step she took, and raised her hand
    To undisguise the glories of her face;
But the same touch unloosed the careless band
    That bound her hair, and quickly from its place
Down her soft neck the laughing tresses flew,
Startling its white with night's contrasted hue.

Then with her glance she keenly searched his eyes,
    To learn what ruler in his heart prevailed;
Love was not there, but only mute surprise,
    Whose icy towers are not by passion scaled;
Her eyes dropped down; her soul its joy forgot;
Faintly she murmured—"Dost thou know me not?"

"Alas! too well; impute it not to me,
    O guardian powers of friendship's holy shrine,
That I have wrought this worst indignity
    To one whose hand hath oft been clasped in mine;
I knew her not; should I be swift to guess
That child of his would tempt my loneliness?

"Alas! poor child, what evil hast thou wrought!
    What end was thine? what didst thou think to gain
When thus thy life untempted, unbesought,
    Laid down its peace to grasp eternal pain?
Amid the pure thou hast no longer part,—
I dare not name thee as the thing thou art.

"And how shall I unguiltily behold
    Thy father's face ? Yea, mine is not the blame ;
But shall his anger suffer to be told
    That thou hast won a twofold crown of shame ?
Thy fault alone hath doomed us ; I must flee
To some far land ; and what remains for thee ? "

As drops the water in some glittering cave,
    And, as it drops, turns all the floor to stone,
So dropped those words upon her soul who gave
    No outward sign that life still held his own ;
She looked not up, nor spake, but only pressed
With clenching hands upon her marble breast.

Had night then come so soon ? Was joy for ever
    Fled from the sky before the south was crossed ?
Was April crowned with snow, and love's sweet river
    Held in the chains of such untimely frost ?
Was there no power which might again unbind
The wandering passions by despair confined ?

Yet words of hope came struggling to the lips
    Of her whose dread awhile had held her dumb ;
Her eyes grew dim, yet not with death's eclipse,
    But with the tears that unresisted come
When life beholds its avenue of years
Lengthening once more beyond some shade of fears.

" O Love,—for mine thou art and mine wilt be,
  When thou hast heard the sorrows of my state,—
Think it no shame that I have brought to thee
  What some might yield to words importunate ;
Or, thinking so, let this my love prevail
To make shame naught, and lift the threatening scale.

" How shall I tell thee when my love began ?
  Lo ! as the clouds grow bright before the day,
When gathering breezes first begin to fan
  That crimson fire which burns the stars away,
So could my heart remain no longer cold
When once mine eyes had ventured to behold.

" Who counts away the progress of a year,
  Or who doth find the gliding seasons long ?
Weary they seem to some lone prisoner
  Whom war hath chained in fortress walls too strong,—
Life-thirsty tyrants, granting no release,
Until they shake before the trump of peace.

"There month by month the southern moonlight
      streams
  Through narrow casements, crossed by many a bar,
And wakes him rudely from a bower of dreams
  To show how false those dreams of freedom are ;
His expectation makes the time more slow,
Yet doth it move ;—ah ! would that mine did so !

" For but a year,—twelve moons that waned and fell,
    One withered Spring, one Autumn's vintage sad,—
Hath passed us by since first I learned to dwell
    Only in that which only makes me glad,—
Only in sweet remembrances of thee ;—
Twelve moons, my love, but each a century.

" Dost thou remember,—haply thou dost not,
    For love alone keeps reckoning of such days,—
When first we met thee in that gardened spot
    To which my father oft at evening strays ?
The chance-dropped speech that held thee chained with him
In close dispute till all the world grew dim ?

" Within my home thou camest,—then I shrank
    Behind the sheltering curtain that o'erhung
Some deep recess, and in concealment drank
    The words that flowed like music from thy tongue ;
Legends of beauty, mysteries of art,
Charming the darkness from my father's heart.

" I heard thee speak of honour,—then I knew
    That for thyself was sounded all thy praise ;
Of constancy,—ah ! truth would not be true
    If fickle change could overcast thy days !
And while I heard, and while my heart approved,
More fervently, more hopelessly, I loved.

" For evermore I saw thee come and go,
    Heeding me not, save with such passing heed
As some high prince might carelessly bestow
    On one who sought deliverance in his need ;
Like some bright star, thy light could shine on me,
But what was I, that I should climb to thee ?

" And oftentimes—forgive me, love, this wrong—
    I thought to tear thy likeness from my heart ;
But the resolve which morn beheld so strong
    At eve rebelled, and took the contrary part ;
And while those twelve sad moons went slowly by,
I fought with life, and yet I could not die.

" But love hath armoury of cunning wiles
    Wherewith to rout the foes of his desire,
Not pointless words or vain uncostly smiles,
    But desperate actions, hardened in the fire,
That needs must pierce the target of their aim,-
Or, turning, wound the hand from which they came.

" I called on him for counsel ; then he said
    (Or was it but the rebel overflow
Of my own heart, that looked on all as dead
    Save when thy glance revived it ? Who shall know ?)
' True love is proved by heedless sacrifice ;
Only the false looks round with wary eyes.

"'If unto him thy soul hath long been given,
　Is not the chief part of thy service done?
Resign him all, and grasp the keys of heaven,
　Which without danger are not to be won;
Far better thus to steal the name of wife,
Than let desire wear out the threads of life.'

"Thus all is told;—Ah! never shall we need
　When many years have watched us, hand in hand,
Treading life's ways, to turn again and read
　The tale of this at whose strange end we stand;
Love shall be ours, but pain shall be forgot,—
Like things not done are things remembered not."

Thus while she spake, like flames that stronger rise
　By the fierce action of their rising heat,
So did her words build up hope's fantasies,
　Until they seemed realities more sweet;
But hope itself, like those material fires,
When kindled high, more speedily expires.

For she had leaned upon a broken reed,
　For she had trusted an unworthy bark,
And sent forth all her merchandise to feed
　The hungry caverns of a sea more dark
Than Adria's gulf when all the stars are gone,
And from the north sweeps down Euroclydon.

"O rich in words," he said, "and rich in wiles,
  How hast thou been so venturously bold
To step beyond the wonted bait of smiles
  Which women use to snare too tempting gold?
How hast thou been so faithless to thy peers
To pour their secrets into willing ears?

"Yea, didst thou deem my honour so renowned?
  Then how, fair guest, should it be linked with thine?
The captive eagle fluttereth near the ground,
  Nor longer soars above the topmost pine;
He could not breast the unsubstantial air;—
So, wed to mine, should thy clipped honour fare.

"High up he sees his old companions wheel,
  Tracing wide circles round the falling sun;
He shakes his plumes, and for a space doth feel
  That life enslaved is worse by far than none;
Yet thinks he on the recompensing good,—
A golden chain, a soft embroidered hood.

"So shalt thou find what thou dost most desire,—
  To look the world down from a throne made high
With wealth, not fame; this just subsiding fire
  Reaps a new strength from thy hypocrisy.
To-night we meet? More sweet shall be thy lips
When now thy heart forsweareth all eclipse."

He left her with a kiss and went his way,
    Wrapped in the garment of that gross delight
Which he puts on who lets his lust betray
    The house of fame to undeserved despite ;
Forecasting still what treasury of charms
The laggard night should convoy to his arms.

He left her with a kiss ; she felt it not,
    Save as the touch of some red-heated brand
That scorched her face, and tingling left the spot
    To which anon she raised an ice-cold hand ;
Again, again,—as if to wipe away
Some seal of guilt that feared the light of day.

Awhile she stood in so perplexed a case
    That frightened life resigned his conscious reign ;
The maddened thickets urged a strange wild race,
    Hunting the thoughts that laboured through her brain ;
Beneath her feet, in concert with her heart,
The ground upheaved with many a sudden start.

But as a storm that all day long hath rolled
    Its cloudy warfare round the world's dark rim,
Draws near at last, with blackness fold on fold,
    What time the sickening sunlight waxes dim ;—
So from the tumult of her nature flies
A quick revenge for love's spurned sacrifice.

Sudden as lightning gleamed the dreadful thought,
    But not like Summer lightning died away ;
Homeward she turned ; her floating hair up-caught
    As if each tress were pregnant with delay ;
And as through darkening streets she swept apace
Each passer turned to mark so wild a face.

Poor in his purse, but prouder in his heart
    Than many sprung from long-descended kings,
A worshipper of love, a priest of art,
    Who bade the canvas speak melodious things,
And yet withal a man that seldom smiled,
Save on the fairness of his only child ;—

Her father dwelt within time-honoured halls,
    By failing scions left untenanted ;
And there his hand had filled the wondering walls
    With pictured woes and legends of the dead ;
His child, he said, alone could mock the tomb,—
She only lived 'mid that sepulchral gloom.

Thither she came, but not, as heretofore,
    With flowers and laughter from the murmuring street ;
A shadow stalked behind her through the door,
    Whispering such things as made her hurrying feet
Fall like the echo of some dismal knell
That bids the listener count his moments well.

Across the marble pavement, as she passed,
   The feeble flickering of a lamp o'erhead
Crept like the radiance of a star,—the last
   Which he beholds whose weedy couch is spread
Amid the wreck of many a bark unknown,
To whose deep grave the storm condemns his own.

And where its gleam was brightest on the wall
   She marked the tumult of a crowd that swayed
As swayed the light,—she marked Virginia fall,
   Her sweet life dropping from the Roman blade,
While all around the silent crowd looked on,
Full of strange eyes and gestures woe-begone.

But now she reached a dim secluded store
   Of rusted swords and armour long unused;
Helmets were there which still true witness bore
   That never knight unvaliantly refused
The blows of battle,—breastplates wrapped in dust,
Dinted or pierced by many a foeman's thrust.

These stayed her not, but, quickly gazing round,
   With shuddering taper lifted up on high,
Swift search she made,—and lo! the prize is found!
   Her trembling fingers grasp it eagerly;—
An antique poniard, marvellously chased,
Haply the guardian of some lady's waist.

A ruby crowned the hilt, a drop of blood
    That seemed to make suggestion to the blade ;
It fixed her glance a moment while she stood
    Testing the point, and for that instant made
Such strange confusion of her fixed intent
That at her feet she dropped hate's instrument.

Clashing it fell ; the echoes murmured "death,"
    And words were uttered from each empty helm ;
Her limbs grew cold as if the north wind's breath
    Had brought fresh winter from his snow-clad realm ;
An instant only,—then she laughed to scorn
The fear from such a slight occasion born.

Bright is each spark that from the contact flies
    Of tempered steel and swift revolving stone ;
Yet fiercer far the sparks that fill the eyes
    Of her who whets her vengeance there alone ;
Who smiles anon, and lets her labour pause,
To mark how speeds the champion of her cause.

The night drops down, and fast the time draws nigh
    When she must crown her purpose with the deed ;
Her labour's offspring scarce delights her eye,
    Yet shall it do good service to her need ;
A weary look across her countenance steals ;
Deeply she sighs ; at last in prayer she kneels.

"O God's sweet Mother, thou whose bleeding heart
    Was stricken through with multitudinous woes,
Who know'st too well the passions which upstart
    Within the bruised imaginings of those
Who see the life once cherished at their breast
Counted as naught, degraded, scorned, oppressed ;—

" O be thou merciful ! for thou dost know
    That for myself I might contrive to bear
This baseless wrong, and let my purchased woe
    With time be made repentance' minister ;
But thou dost know that there is one beside
Whose wrong may not thus unavenged abide.

" I ask not pardon for my chief offence,—
    I dare not ask, lest thus my doom increase,
Lest old desire should vanquish penitence,
    And mock the tears that seemed to sue for peace ;
Ah ! let my love my free acquittance gain,
For it 'twas sin, no grace can hide the stain.

" But I this night must darken all my hate
    With love's disguise, must recompense his scorn
Through such deceit as makes me desolate—
    The false, false flower that hid so sharp a thorn ;
If it be so, that I with him must die,
O then forgive my forced hypocrisy ! "

Then to the portal noiselessly she passed,
    A gliding phantom from the graves of eld;
Yet as she went a stealthy look she cast
    Within a door half open, and beheld
Her father sleeping coldly, 'mid the waste
Of used materials thrown aside in haste.

Before his feet the calm resemblance stood,
    Fresh from the last fond touches of his hand,
Of some sweet saint, whose spotless maidenhood
    Had sought death's kindly friendship to withstand
The rude assaults of those who watched her rise,
Drawn from the earth 'mid heavenly companies.

Ah! 'twas her own sweet face that gazed at her
    From off that canvas indistinctly seen!
Her own sweet face, before this new despair
    Had made her youth as though it had not been!
Her heart beat quick;—"It shall not live," she said,
"To mock my woes when I, perchance, am dead."

Still noiselessly within the door she stepped,
    And from her breast the fateful weapon drew;
From top to base the murderous sentence crept,
    To right and left the yielding canvas flew;
And, as it yielded, hoarse complaining sent
To him whose toil was then declared misspent.

But he waked not, and not a whisper moved
　The shades that crouched beneath each silent wall ;
And for herself, how much soe'er she loved,
　'She dared not speak,—a look must serve for all,—
For all that drawn out action of farewell
Which will not heed Time's warning sentinel.

Soon had she reached the dim deserted square,
　(For lukewarm passion only moveth slow) ;
Too soon, perchance ; a while she lingered there,
　Watching the moonlight gently come and go
Upon each marble pinnacle and spire
That decked the shrine of many a heart's desire.

Above the silent darkness of the street
　Like some huge Alp rose up the glimmering pile,
Whiter and ever whiter to the feet
　Of saints that crowned each buttress of the aisle ;
And over all in milky splendour hung
The traceried dome, wherein each anthem sung

Wanders and wanders like a soul that seeks
　Some outlet from a region too confined,
Testing each pane through which at evening breaks
　A glory by the daylight left behind
What time it sinks beyond the westward plain,
And o'er the city night declares her reign.

It was a sight to make the wounded whole,
   To end in peace the spirit's turbulence,
And even to hers some gentler influence stole
   That seemed in act to drive destruction thence ;
A touch, a whispered greeting in her ear,
And hate resumed his regency of fear.

Yea ! comes unwarned the quarry to the net ?
   Is there no foam which to the seaman's eye
Reveals the ridge in expectation set
   Beneath the ocean's tranquil majesty ?
Is there no teaching even in her breath ?
Are not her kisses pregnant with his death ?

But his desire had blinded all his sense,—
   Desire by that Lethean wine made strong
Wherewith he sought to dull the eloquence
     Of restless thoughts that charged himself with wrong :
Through the strait alleys silently they glide ;—
So guilt and vengeance travel side by side.

O midnight ! thou art glorious for thy dress
   Of solemn blue, whose star-wove harmonies
Compass the world that casts its weariness
   Westward each morning as the day-beams rise ;
Thou hast enchantment for the soul's unrest,
And plaining lips in sleep declare thee blest.

O midnight! thou art dreadful for thy crown
   Of dark offence, for many a helpless cry,
For many a wreck that slowly drifteth down
   Upon the reefs of opportunity!
Thou hast destruction for the soul's despair,
That calls thee still its readiest minister.

Now did she wake whose feignéd sleep had snared
   The unsuspecting victim of her hate;
Listening awhile, no other sound she heard
   Save the deep breath that knelled his gathering fate;
Close to his face anon she held her own,—
Touched his pale brow, and yet it passed unknown.

Then did one hand, while over him she knelt,
   Draw forth the steel so quickly to be stained
With death's red vintage, while the other felt
   Where still his heart its easy pace maintained;
Her right arm from its drapery she freed,
Lest for his life its touch should intercede.

About her face in supplication fell
   Each frighted tress that dared not watch him die,
And o'er her breast wherein began to dwell
   The sweet strange thoughts of young maternity;
Yet did she thrust them scornfully aside,—
O love! is now thine anger satisfied?

For she hath overstepped that narrow line
    Which parteth chance from direful certainty ;
The gates are burst, and empty lies the shrine
    Wherein was planned her lasting infamy ;
Quenched are life's tapers, all the chorus fled,
And soon the roof will crumble overhead.

Yet as she gazed 'twas hard to understand
    How Death had made his sudden entrance there ;
Only a start, a clenching of the hand
    That late had found its pastime midst her hair ;
Could such be all the witness of that strife
Wherein destruction overmatches life ?

O strange revenge ! O self-consuming fire !
    That burnest fiercely, hearkening not to prayer,
Then dost thyself more suddenly expire,
    Leaving but ashes of unsweet despair !
How dost thou mock the narrow sense of those
Who think from thee to purchase their repose !

Ah ! could she but have e'er so faintly guessed,
    Before her purpose to the act had grown,
That the same steel which quartered in his breast
    Would dispossess the tyrant of her own,—
That the same hour wherein he ceased to live
Would see her passion's mystery revive ;—

He had not died; but what remaineth now?
   Would she dissolve death's frost in burning tears?
Could thousand kisses flush that marble brow,
   Or thousand words make quick those heedless ears?
Yet every sign that showed her prayers were vain
Became a spur to urge them forth again.

Then grief grew dumb, and many hours she lay,
   Clasping him dead whom living she had spurned,
Till through the casement streamed a cold faint gray,
   To supersede the lamp that dimly burned
With such a pale and undetermined light
As seemed to speak the horrors of the night.

Then, as the rush of one tremendous wave
   Splits up the wreck already sorely tried,
Startling the hollows of each shoreward cave
   With shrieks of death that tremble and subside;
So did renewed observance give the lie
To each fond hope of unreality.

Only one look and one long passionate kiss,
   Only one sob that summed up all her woe,
And after his across the drear abyss
   Her soul had fled; the daylight's early glow
Looked through the panes and might have deemed they slept,
Save for the purple rivulet that crept,—

That slowly crept from her invaded side
   Around the base of love's deserted hills,
To feed a lake whose slow-congealing tide
   Seemed like the fence of their divided wills ;—
Of hers, whose love became a wasting fire,—
Of his, whose death revived her slain desire.

THE BEACON.

Upon the topmost height I stand,
    Where breezes wander free ;
A sea-mark to the bordering land,
    A landmark to the sea.

I trace beneath the lanes that twine
    By cottage, field, and farm ;
I hear the lowing of the kine,
    The sheep-bell's tinkling charm.

I hear at times the church bells sound,
    And watch the straggling files
Converge from all the hamlets round
    To fill the mouldering aisles.

I see where calmly rest the dead,
    Each in his grave alone ;
Ah ! would that I could stoop my head
    To kiss one sacred stone !

For where the wild Aurora shines
    On fiord and trackless snow,
Even there, amid Norwegian pines,
    Some centuries ago,—

My tender crest burst through the ground;
    There waxed I straight and tall,
Until ambition saw me crowned
    The sovereign pine of all.

And upward still I thought to shoot,
    Toward heaven, many an ell;
But lo! the axe was at my root,
    And in the stream I fell.

In blinding sheets the foam was dashed
    Far up each rocky wall;
Through whizzing rapids down I crashed,
    Through roaring waterfall.

Ah! woe was I to leave behind
    The land I loved so well!
The sighing of the prisoned wind
    In reindeer-haunted dell;

The north at midnight all ablaze
    With fiery darts and streams;
The long, long nights, the long, long days,
    The summer dawn of dreams.

And oft, as still we swirled along,
  I stretched my branches wide
To clasp some rock, but still too strong
  I found the swollen tide.

Ah! memory, wilt thou ne'er forsake
  A time too fraught with woe?
Perchance 'twas well that leave to take
  Round half the world to go.

For in a tall, stout Indiaman
  Was straightway stepped my heel;
Swift past her sides the salt seas ran,
  And gurgled round her keel.

What need to tell the course we went?
  What need at length to say
How sails were split and spars were bent
  As sped the months away?

What needs my little skill to speak
  Of strange East Indian isles,
Or Teneriffe, whose sea-girt peak
  Is watched for miles on miles?

What need to speak of calms that wrought
  Corruption on the main,
Till, with the swiftness of a thought,
  Uprose the hurricane?

A stranger tale have I to tell—
   A tale that moves me still,
And saddens every Sabbath bell
   That sounds beneath the hill.

O cruel was that night of grief,
   And fierce the north wind blew!
But fiercer was the foaming reef
   That pierced our timbers through!

O loud and louder shrieked the blast!
   But not so loud its cry
As theirs who knew that night their last,
   And prayed, yet feared to die.

O hard and harder smote the seas,—
   The ship was slow to part;
Yet not so slow as hope did freeze
   In each despairing heart.

Amid the calmer shoals I swung
   Beneath her sheltering lee,
And many were the souls that hung
   Their naked lives on me.

O longer than the longest day
   Death's bitterness they drank!
But one by one they dropped away,
   And one by one they sank.

And I was left,—not all alone,
   For to my side was bound
One life, more costly than their own
   Who saved it ere they drowned.

O hast thou seen the tender green
   That clothes some mouldering wall?
So did she cling, a helpless thing,
   That only saved of all.

Did'st e'er thou creep and softly peep
   Where snugly sits the wren?
So did she rest her childish breast
   Upon my bosom then.

And once methought I felt her move,
   And once I heard her pray,
And once the name that children love
   Went from her lips astray.

But cold and heartless was the north,
   And icy cold the sea;
From her sweet lips her soul went forth,
   And entered into me.

(Ay! into me; I feel it thrill,
   In these long-after times,
Through all my bulk, when up the hill
   Come faint the Sabbath chimes.)

Her spirit entered into me,
   And silently I prayed
That nevermore on such a sea
   Might such a life be laid.

They brought us slowly to the beach ;
   I saw the wreckers' eyes
Drop tears more eloquent than speech
   For such a tender prize.

They laid her where the grass waves long,
   And where the stones are grey ;
I saw, well pleased, the village throng
   To honour her that day.

They laid her in the sweet churchyard,
   And long untouched I lay
Upon the sand, so smooth and hard,
   That curves round all the bay.

And there the children came at noon,
   The fishers came at eve,
And there at night, beneath the moon,
   I saw the ground swell heave.

But evermore I prayed in heart
   (Or was it she that prayed ?)
That nevermore a ship might part
   Where that brave keel was laid.

And I was heard : for here I stand,
　Where every wind is free,
A silent preacher to the land,
　A safeguard to the sea.

Far off I watch the sails go by,
　And many a thankful prayer,
Entwined with many an exile's sigh,
　Floats to me through the air.

With eyes of joy I watch them pass,
　Yet scarce my heart is moved ;
O rather flies it to the grass
　Where rests the child I loved !

O tenfold rather on the sea
　Would I be wandering now,
With those small hands enfolding me,
　Than on this windy brow !

O rather far !—for no man knows
　Her name, and time doth roll
Strange mists about her oft-told woes ;
　But is not mine her soul ?

'Tis thus I lightly speak at times,
　But then I hear once more
Reproval in the far, faint chimes
　Or in the storm's great roar.

And when around these crumbling steeps
   The swell begins to stir,
I murmur to myself, "She sleeps
   Where none can trouble her!"

TWO RIVERS.

Across the plain, beneath the shimmering sky,
   Beyond the sails slow drifting with the stream,
Soars up the matchless milk-white canopy—
   A stone-wrought symphony, a marble dream.

Love built it—love, such love as kings can feel,
   With whom nor stint nor limit may control
One heart-felt wish; whose hatreds pierce like steel,
   Who, when they love, love with unbounded soul.

Love built it—love, that mightier than death,
   In sure remembrance of the radiant queen
Who to imperial precept lent the breath
   Of tempering mercy, whose eclipse had been

The blotting out of gladsomeness, the theft
   Of life's best jewel from an emperor's crown,
The gems of fame and far dominion left,
   But from the heart all light and glory flown.

As loved, so mourned ; as honoured, so proclaimed
   Most worthy all that might through time illume
The memory of a soul so chastely framed,
   Peerless in life, still peerless in the tomb.

As thought, so willed ; for that imperious love
   Bade Western art with Eastern fancy wed
To weave a priceless canopy above
   Where death smiles strangely o'er a nuptial bed.

And all around, where mazy gardens lie,
   By fountains fed and far from worldly fret,
The cypress waves, and thousand odours vie
   To breathe the incense of a world's regret.

And the cool wave from Himalayan snows
   Flecks its clear breast with many a marble gleam,
Drinking warm scents of roses as it goes
   Down to its marriage with the Sacred Stream.

Love reigns remembered ; yet no sceptre's sway
   Here centres now ; no power ordains, condemns ;
Change yields to change, and history seeks to-day
   The soul of empire by the embowered Thames.

And that fair Eastern river, gliding on
   Through Winter's drought or Summertime's increase,
Amid the memories of a rule bygone,
   Breathes to his Western brother words of peace.

"Just laws, firm peace, the poor man's bread secure,
　Pale Famine scotched, and hungry Death subdued,
These are the gifts of empire that endure,
　The gems that crown a king's beatitude.

"These things endure; yet with them alway dwells
　The chilling sense of self-preserving care;
Clear is the draught drawn up from wisdom's wells,
　But love's fresh fount is thousandfold more fair.

"These things endure; yet, more eternal far,
　Shall the rich love that raised this peerless fane
Shine with the glory of an orient star
　When the last empire trembles to its wane."

And Thames made answer, all his woodland deeps
　Stirred as by breaths from dew-filled darkness drawn
When the first touch of faintest crimson peeps
　Above the shoulder of the listening dawn.

"Wisdom is marble; love like burning fire;
　Love sought out marble for a love's last home;
That choice was well; but love hath chosen higher
　When wisdom's self crowns the memorial dome.

"High art was his who carved the traceried pier;
　Deep love was that which nerved the sculptor's tool;
But deeper love and loftier art reign here,
　Where love builds up a monument of rule.

"To strengthen justice with imperial power,
    To guard for toil the labour of its hands,
To snatch the sting from Famine's threatening hour,
    To bind in peace the hopes of scattered lands :—

" These are such works as vanquish the pretence
    Of power self-sought for bitter greed of gain,—
The quenchless light of high benevolence
    Linked with the splendour of unrivalled reign.

" Nor this alone ; for fame shall blazon most,
    Far through the years by human history spanned,
How, in the waste of bleak bereavement lost,
    The woman's heart inspired the regal hand.

" Dead are these memories of the Eastern dead ;
    Silent the vault, the marble cold above ;
Here in the West the world beholds outspread,
    In living deeds, the warmth of wifely love."

So Thames ; and straightway o'er his breast there flew
    A breeze all moist with gleanings from the main ;
The stream turned dark, and all the woodlands through
    Swept the soft murmur of the Summer rain.

Grey gloom for gladsomeness ; but soon the shower
    Passed eastward ; to the meadows one by one
Light coming back, and o'er a rounded tower
    A broad bright standard floating in the sun.

A BRIDAL SONG.

[*July* 6, 1893.]

PRINCESS, and you that with her come
    To be, within this time-worn isle
Where not a throat of joy seems dumb,
    The lode-star of an Empire's smile ;—

Fear not, when loud the trumpets blow
    And welcome fills the thronging street,
Fear not to entertain the glow
    Of life's best promise made complete.

No wound is felt by him who sleeps
    Uncrowned amid the regal dead ;
Yea, rather, from some mystic deeps
    In silent joy his hands are spread.

Nor recks he that untimeous fate
    Has willed it that another now
May claim that diadem of State
    Which birthright traced about his brow.

For who shall tell, the world forgot,
    If gain be loss, or loss be gain,—
If best to emulate his lot
    Whose wisdom scotched the fiery Dane :—

Or best to praise the unsullied steel,
    The broken dream of noblest things,
Of him whose valour bade him kneel
    The servitor of vanquished kings?

We know not; yet beyond all guess
    We know that with that kingly soul
A thought of self avails far less
    Than care for England's regal goal.

But you, whose glory makes ascent
    From that dark lake where dipped its wing,
Whose name in million hearts is blent
    With England's fairest gift of Spring;—

And you, well rendering for the State,
    Due service to her sea-borne brand,—
That guardian of our Eden's gate
    Which Alfred forged for Nelson's hand;—

Even you, to whom the years have brought,
    Unasked, so mystical a chain,
A bond in tears and darkness wrought,
    A love made deep by partnered pain;—

A BRIDAL SONG.

Even you, for whom the trumpets blare,
   You, whom ten million throats as one,
Cannon accompanied, declare
   Fresh bulwarks of an Empire's throne :—

What hope for you shall best be breathed ?
   For which be prayed increasing grace
Of all the countless gifts bequeathed
   By act or birth, by time or race ?

So much to win, so much to dread ;
   Yet, Princess, to your hand may come
A charm more certain than the thread
   Which brought the Attic tribute home.

Take only this—the woman's heart
   That, when a score of thrones went down
At Titan Europe's wakening start,
   Redeemed the light of England's crown.

Take only this, a queenlike dower,
   Nor doubt that, while the years abide,
Translated into manhood's power,
   It lives in him who calls you bride.

So freighted, glide, O happy ship,
   Glide forth while skies and winds are fair,
With golden praise on every lip,
   In every heart a silent prayer.

Glide forth o'er shoal, o'er surging deep,
  Still moving toward a vaster sea,
Borne by the mighty thoughts that keep
  The heart of England warm and free.

A SOUTHERN CHRISTMAS.

FLOATING above the milk-white walls
  That mark the verge of Albion's isle,
Above the furrowed sea, where crawls
  The home-bound trader,—mile on mile
Through the chill air the sounds are borne
Of chimes that wake the Christmas morn.

And fainter yet, on ice-tipped breeze,
  Spurning the vintaged fields of France,
They touch the breast of azure seas
  That wreathe the shores of old romance;
And like a wandering dream impinge
On northern Afric's Moslem fringe.

Faint and more faint through quivering haze
  That wraps the wide Sahara's plain,
Lost in the tangled tropic maze
  Of stream and forest, once again
They waken with a voice that seems
Like quaint old carols, heard in dreams.

Only in dreams,—so changed the sky,
  So distant all that breathes of home,
That even listening brings a sigh,
  So fruitlessly those echoes come.
No, let the passing fancy fade ;—
Warring with facts, dreams bring no aid.

    *   *   *   *   *

Ah ! not in vain, ye Christmas chimes,
  Your echoes wander round the world,
For Northern wrath and Northern crimes
  Still track the flag that flies unfurled
Wherever dark blue surges roll
Past capes that watch the southward pole.

More prone to strike, less quick to feel
  The sweetness of a just desire,
Hard circumstance becomes our steel,
  And fear the flint from which a fire
Is struck in haste, and mourned in pain
When loss outweighs the fancied gain.

Less quick to feel,—yet not too slow
  When clear-eyed reason laughs at dread,
And even perforce commends the foe
  Whose spear once laid our kinsman dead ;—
Nor time can quench, nor flame, nor flood,
The Saxon justice in our blood.

O Child of Peace ! whose welcome rings
   This morn from thousand village fanes,
Across the holly'd copse that flings
   Its shelter over wintry lanes,—
Across the fields, whose pathways lead
To joy the quick, to rest the dead :—

Whose wandering and mysterious star
   Stood fixed in heaven that happy night
When woman's pain and man's deep care
   Gave place to strange, unknown delight,
As, while they watched, that first-born Child
Gazed on a troublous world—and smiled :—

O Child of Peace ! in that far isle
   From age to age beloved by all
Whose youth in years, or youth in guile,
   Can meet, unshamed, thy festival,—
Come from that ice-bound northern sphere,—
Come, for we surely need thee here !

Come with the mirth of childhood's pleasure,
   Come with the tears of childhood's woe ;
The generous heart that knows not measure,
   The grasp of friends, the cheeks that glow
As by the light of love's pure story
Life's very thorns seem touched with glory.

Come with the wealth of wrongs forgiven,
    Of peace made sure for vengeance vowed ;
Memories of saints, like scents from heaven
    Dropped from some wandering April cloud :
Here bites no frost, nor hollies twine,
Yet even here the world is thine.

Here in the dim South gleams the Cross ;
    Here in the Orient shines the Crown ;
Patience may find its gain in loss,
    And love that diadem'd renown
Which, from her stormy strife of years,
The sad-eyed Europe proudly wears.

So come, so touch us ; not when dark
    The storm-cloud wraps the rifted hills,
And broad and bright the purple spark
    Gleams in the myriad foam-wreath'd rills ;
Not when the fierce sun checks his march
High in the noontide's fiery arch.

But when, from eves of fruitful rains,
    The night mists slowly lift and rise,
And cool and moist the silent plains
    Lie dim beneath the dawn-touched skies ;
When streams across the eastern bar
A flood submerging star by star :—

A flood of soft and kindling light
    That wakes the hill-tops one by one,
And paves with gold the pathway bright
    By which climbs up the hastening sun ;
When the tall blue-gum gently stirs,
And faint scents float from slumbering firs :—

When, 'mid the hush that makes more clear
    The sound of streams about its foot,
The table'd mount shows sharp and near,
    Gazing, immovable and mute,
Into the still blue depth above,—
A silent Sinai crowned with Love.

OUTSPANNED.

The evening falls; stands still the labouring wain;
    Far o'er the veldt the long-horned oxen stray;
A faint breeze stirs, then faintly dies again,
    And silence seals the obsequies of day.

Wide spreads the plain, and wider still the sky
    Stoops o'er it like a vast and shoreless sea,
Dew-filled and deep, in whose recesses lie
    Faint star-like visions of futurity.

Beside the wheel the ruddy embers glow;
    The smoke curls up; the wanderer's simple fare
Scant art requires; the sparks die out, and lo!
    All things are wrapped in sleep's considerate care.

Great stars climb up to mark the hour, and fall
    Into the dew-drenched dimness of the west;
No sound, except some night-bird's distant call,
    Invades the stillness of pervading rest.

Ah! yet, methinks, through other nights than this
   Toiled weary teams across the houseless plain,
When flame and thunder mingled with the hiss
   Of hurrying waters, late arrears of rain.

Far other nights, far other days they knew
   Who, in the times by grandsires scarce recalled,
Forsook loved homes, and to the wilds withdrew
   To shun the flag, to quit the rule that galled.

No land of promise called them; all that wore
   The smile of hope lay in those desolate fields;
Their welcome met them in the lion's roar,
   The quivering dart, the din of warlike shields.

Here the coiled snake his murderous venom nursed,
   Here lurked destruction in the perilous ford,
Stones mocked at hunger, drought replied to thirst,
   Death's frown in front,—behind, the half-drawn sword.

Strangers and pilgrims, worn, yet undismayed,
   Brave to endure, and braver to submit,
Seeking a city, from the past they strayed
   Into a future cavernous and unlit.

Vague forms, vague hopes around them,—nothing sure,
   Save that each day unfailingly must see
Its threats of death, its conflict to secure
   Some slender staff for life's necessity.

Yet faith was theirs, and strength, by will Divine,
   To pierce through gross obscurity, to smite
Powers of darkness, striving to enshrine
   The rule of mercy for the rule of might ;—

To plant the seed of governance, to spread
   The light of order through untravelled lands,
To see fair peace with stalwart justice wed,
   And homes made fruitful by laborious hands.

And we their children,—children or by birth,
   Or by acceptance of their toils and tears,—
Put forth our powers to garner from the earth
   The golden harvest of unfolding years.

For us they laboured, suffered, died, endured ;
   For us their homes abandoned, for our weal
The rest by blood-stained sacrifice procured,
   The plough converted to the warrior's steel.

The rose-bud blossoms where their wheels rolled by ;
   Here stand, memorial of their arduous days,
Cities to dwell in, founts that run not dry,
   High roads from which no simple wanderer strays.

For us they laboured ; we their toils fulfil ;
   We, not ungrateful as the years unroll,
Possess the realm which their unyielding will
   Carved from the waste and kindled with a soul.

Each scene recalls them,—when the storm-cloud
    stoops
  Upon the thunderous ridges, when the plain
Shimmers with heat, or to the flower that droops
  God's benediction comes in showers of rain.

Or when, through dawn-gleams stealthily increased,
  Faint and more faint each constellation burns,
Till white-robed morning broadens in the east,
  And to the yoke the slow-paced ox returns.

A SONG OF PEACE.*

Only a patter of hail,
   A patter of hail in the street;
And a flash and a peal from an angry cloud
   In the hush of the noontide heat;
Only a patter of hail,
   And the cloud had broken and gone,
And the hills lay bright in the broad cool light
   Till the long, long day was done.

Only a whisper of war,—
   A cloud in a clearing sky,—
Only a whisper of war
   As the days of doubt went by;
Only a fear and a frown,
   And the fear had broken and passed,
And the frown gave place to the soft sweet grace
   Of a peace made sure at last.

               * See Note.

A SONG OF PEACE.

There were children in Warwickshire lanes,
    As the Autumn days grew dull,
Who asked if yet there were words of hope,—
    If the tale of death was full;
There were children, and mothers who prayed
    Till the day was one long desire;
Till an angel's hand in a far off land
    Flashed "Peace!" through the trembling wire.

And the Boer, come back to his farm,
    Went forth with the dawning day;
But his eye grew dim ere the shot rang out,
    And the springbok bounded away;
He shouldered his gun with a smile;
    The children went hungry to bed;
But they talked of peace through the light's decrease,
    And dreamed of one that was dead.

And the chiefs in a thousand kraals
    From the far faint lakes to the sea,
Laid down their dreams of a rule to come
    In a kingdom yet to be;
There was joy, they said, in the bayonet's gleam,
    There was hope in the cannon's roar;
But a firm sure hand of strength in the land
    Where the white man wars no more.

A SONG OF PEACE.

O come, with thy heats and storms,
    Come, Summer, across the hills,
Wash out the blood with a stronger flood
    Than fell in our year of ills !
Wash out the old year's distrust,—
    The slavish taint from the free,—
The canker of scorn between races born
    On the marge of the northern sea.

Fall, fall, where the corn-shoot springs,
    Where the long-horned oxen graze,
On the sheep-trod veldt, on the plains that melt
    In the weird equatorial haze ;
Fall, fall, where the golden globes
    Gleam out from the dark-leaved bowers,
Where the cane waves bright, and the soft warm night
    Is faint with the scents of flowers.

Fall, rains, till the earth grows full
    With the fruits of a land that is free,
Bring hands to toil, and the plough to the soil,
    And the ship to the bustling quay ;
And whisper, in gentler voice,
    Over dark Amajuba's sod,
That the wrath of man may rage and plan,
    But Peace is the will of God !

CARMEN SOLARE.

We praise thee, we praise thee, we praise thee,
Our life and our strength and our gladness;
We praise thee, the giver of good
To all things that move under heaven;
We praise thee unrivalled in glory,
We praise thee unbounded in power,
We praise thee unchanged and eternal,
Though man in his numberless races
Should pass from thy face as a mist
And the name of his place be forgotten.

We praise thee, for thine is the forest,
And thine is the moss by the stream,
The cedar that shadows the mountain,
The lichen that covers the rock;
Yea, and the beast that feedeth,
The insect that flies through the evening,
All that have life and have breath,
All, even we, are thy children;
Thine are the lilies, and thine
The verdure of wide-spreading pastures,
The flocks and the cattle that roam
Uncounted o'er numberless hills.

We labour, but thine is the strength ;
We are glad, but our health is from thee ;
Yea, thine are the thoughts of our hearts,
And the night with its visions of wonder.
We praise thee, yet tremble before thee ;
For thine, even thine, is the power
Of sudden destruction that dwells
In the lightning that strikes and is seen not,
In the fury of wind-driven surges,
In the fleetness and rage of the lion,
In the terrible spring of the panther ;
Yea, when the eagle upsoars,
Or slideth the snake through the tangle,
Thine is the eagle's flight,
Thine also the wave of the serpent.

Thine is the growth of the forest,
Thine also the stroke of the woodman ;
The grass springeth up in thy strength,
In thy strength is cut down by the mower ;
Thine is the gold of the merchant,
And thine is the sword of the warrior ;
We vanquish the deep in thy might,
And time in the strength of thy power ;
Thou givest us food for our health
And clothing for the cold of the winter ;
Thine is the toil of our hands,
The forge and the anvil and hammer.

The tide of thy glory pours forth,
On every side it is passing ;
Here, on this earth which we quit not,
A few drops only descending
Call into being each moment
Ten million lives and sustain them ;
Here, though formless thou art,
Bodiless, spirit of spirit,
In bodily shape thou revealest
Something awhile of thy glory,
Something to those whom thou givest
Power to look for and see it.
All things from thee proceeding,
All things to thee returning,
Taking what shape thou wilt give them,
Living awhile in thy pleasure,
Dying when thou dost command them,—
All things, O bountiful giver,
Speak forth thy praises for ever ;
All things, and we with our lips
For ever, and ever, and ever.

MOLOCH.

Under the sod they laid him in a grave with a thousand more,
Under the sod still drenched with the blood-red rain of war;
Even his name forgotten, if ever his name was known;
He stood but now in the ranks, and the cannon found its own.

Say, were there those far off who twined a prayer with his name?
Say, had he nobly dreamed of the shining laurels of fame?
Shattered that golden dream, unanswered that tender prayer,—
Only the sod on his breast, and the soldier's farewell in the air.

Was there a woman who mused in the silent depths of the night
On the life that lay quick within and the joy that should bring it to light?
Was there a mother who smiled at the small soft face at her breast,
Or bent with a whispered prayer at eve o'er the cradled nest?

Once were there tottering steps that turned to the outstretched arm?
Once were there words half lisped in the fulness of childhood's charm?
Once were there wayward tears, or the touch of the penitent's kiss,—
Love budding forth with the years, and hope like a garden of bliss?

The yearning earth cried out—" Give, give me the hands of toil!
My children wait to be born from the womb of the teeming soil!"
The cannon boomed forth in reply, and slaughter broke forth like a flood,
And the roots and the leaves of the grass were stained with the toiler's blood!

O Moloch! imperial-crowned, high-priested by prelates and peers,
Athirst for the glory of blood, unmoved by importunate tears,
Rewarding the slayer of thousands with bauble of title or star,
And drowning the cry of the slain with the trumpet-tongued pæans of war;—

O Moloch! how long shalt thy worship draw babes from the pitiful breast
To pass through thy furnace of fury, still deeming the sacrifice blest?
To breathe forth their lives for a fancy, to find themselves ruined and left
With the groan of the earth that lies wasted, the cry of the mothers bereft?

Behold! as the calm slays the tempest, as the vine-cluster wanders and clings
O'er the rock that was rent by the earthquake, as the grass o'er the trophies of kings,
As the weak things of God and of nature prevail o'er the forces of might,
So the Moloch of empire shall vanish, and strength be the servant of right.

So the Moloch of empire shall perish; but woe to the merciless strong
Who purchase with blood and with weeping the right to prevail in the wrong!
The cloud-gates of time close behind them on the depths of the endless unknown,
Where their shades flit through darkness for ever, defiled with the crimes of a throne!

GRIEF'S FOUNTAIN.

The world is full of sorrows ; day by day
    Fresh troops of pilgrims stoop themselves to drink
    From that strange fountain, whose unequal brink
With tread of countless steps is worn away ;
Eager are some, and some can scarce convey
    Their faint limbs to the margin, where they sink ;
    And some there are who vainly strive to think
That through that pool Lethean waters stray.
But who may count their numbers, who foretell
    How many thence shall bear a lightening load,
How many seek the desperate gates of hell ?
    How many, born for joy but ill-bestowed,
Shall journey onwards, deeming all is well,
    And die, worn out, upon the weary road ?

WATCHING.

Watching for morning, the night dropped away;
  The blackness turned darkness, the darkness turned gray;
The gray paled to amber that deepened to red,—
  Then up came the sunrise, and buried his dead.

Watching for morning, the night dropped away;
  Despair found a glimmer that taught it to pray;
Then hope changed to gladness, and faith became flame,
  And joy looked on life through a curtain of shame.

Watching for morning, the night drops away;
  But where is the amber, or where is the gray?
O is there no prophet to lesson our eyes,
  And read us the wisdom that looks from the skies?

Watching for morning, the night drops away;—
  The night is around thee, within thee the day;
And if from the amber thou look for the red,
  Move on with the living, and bury thy dead.

DECLINING DAY.

I know not what of sadness or of pain
   Touches the spirit, while from this mute height
   We watch the shortening day recall his light
From dreamy flats, and more uncertain main ;
Whether it be that childhood wakes again,
   From too protracted slumber, at the sight
   Of its beloved consoler, whether night
Brings hints of limit to the labouring brain,—
How best decide ? Yet always unto me
   This sad soft moment hath the power to raise
All thoughts of life from their finality
   Into an arch based far beyond the haze
   Where in the east the lingering moonlight stays,
And far beyond the rising line of sea.

A DAGGER.

What is the sheath?   An outward mien
   All gemmed with friendly show,
In whose bright sparkling is not seen
   The death that lurks below.

The handle, what?   A fair pretence
   That for the grasp is framed
So well that no recoiling sense
   Can mar the blow once aimed.

What is the hilt?   A guarded skill
   The time to understand,
Lest through some haste a kindred ill
   Should touch the striker's hand.

And what the blade, whose gleaming spark
   Is crossed by many a stain?
Revenge that striketh in the dark,
   Nor needs to strike again.

BEN LEDI.

(From the Colinton Road, Edinburgh.)

WHAT art thou, faint and solitary hill
    That in the far-off distance, like a tower
    Stand'st bathed in light, while here with falling shower
The afternoon beholds us battling still?
What art thou, say? And whence the thoughts that fill
    Me, gazing at thee in this silent hour
    As if in contemplation of a power
That bends each adverse influence to its will?
Are there, in truth, heroic thoughts that climb,
    By ways of sense, within the sanctuary
Of inmost being, prompting acts sublime?
    Or is the strength that seems enthroned in thee
A reflex of the bitter fruits of time,
    That shadows forth my own necessity?

A DIAMOND.

Born 'mid the earth's great torments of eruption,
    Flung like a bubble from the unfathomed gloom,
From the corrupt made pure in incorruption,
    A sunbeam treasured in a cosmic tomb ;—

Grasped at by greed, by reckless toil discovered,
    Or by the hands that writhe in slavery's chain,
To be the guerdon of a love unlovered,
    To opiate conscience with the gilt of gain.

Was it for this the travail of creation
    Raged through the waste of vague uncertain form?
Was it for this that peace, by slow gradation,
    Smiled on the wreck of million years of storm?

Yet as, in Time, the harlot's purchased glitter
    Lies but one step from nature's cosmic pains,
So, in the Infinite, what souls find bitter
    Has part with all that boundless space contains.

WHY SEEK YE THE LIVING?

WHY seek ye thus the living midst the dead?
   Why seek the truth that lights, the love that warms,
   'Mid the dry dust of long sepultured forms,
The chills of doubt, the gloom where vaguely tread
Shapes, scarcely seen, of days long vanishéd,
   Changing, ungraspable as mist that swarms
   Athwart the stars, what time autumnal storms
Gather in silence round the Summer's bed?
Why seek ye thus the living? Lo! the day
   Is bright around us! Lo! the self-same Power
That rocked earth's cradle holds us in its sway;
   God walks with us, as once in Eden's hour.
Look up, look round! Through sunshine lies our way
   To where, far off, Love's living domes up-tower!

A SERENADE.

My love retires;
  Her vestal lamp is seen
 Through casements edged with sheltering green,
More steady, yet more faint than marshland fires.

  (O reckless heart!
   What matters it to thee
  That four cold walls alone may see
A beauty past all subtleties of art?)

   O now draw near,
  Music, and clothe her thought
 With sound more soft, more deftly wrought
Than any garments which her white limbs wear.

   (O heavy woe!
   That but with music's lips
  I speak with thee! O vile eclipse,
When wilt thou cease to cross my passion so?)

A SERENADE.

Now, music, die,
And let her spirit fall
Into a reverie so magical
That dawn alone shall break it with a sigh.

(And where go I?
Whether to restless sleep,
Or restless wandering, where the deep
Moans hoarsely to the unregarding sky?)

A CHANGE OF WIND.

As when endurance of some fixed intent,
    Stern with the sense of needful sacrifice,
    Hath made a springless desert of those eyes
Which weep no more except the heart relent ;
And as at length, when all delay seems spent,
    Some thought, begotten of the hope that lies
    Beneath the soul's despairing agonies,
Brings morning joy to night's astonishment ;
So the warm West leads on its wakening power
    Against the East, so bids the proud sky bring
A month's late tribute to this conquering hour ;
    The earth moves round, a new-created thing,
The grass leaps straight beneath the pressing shower,
    And my heart enters on another Spring.

THE VESTAL.

THE river flows through meads that bear
    Red roses on their hem,
All flowers which God hath planted there,—
    God's children gather them.

Yet came there one who did not seem
    In quest of such a crown;
She found a lily by the stream,
    And laid the roses down.

And presently she walked no more
    Amid the festal crew,
But melted to the farther shore
    By ways which no man knew.

"Come back, come back," the children said,
    "And gather in thy right!"
But the pale lily round its head
    Shook out a golden light.

And evermore, by night or day,
    Its soft reflection lies
Across the wide and watery way
    That girdles Paradise.

HOPE IN PARTING.

Not with a tear, nor a half-vanquished sigh,
  Not with a smile, nor any terms of speech,
  Was it made known that henceforth, each to each,
Round half the world's vast bulk our souls should cry;
But like the first gleam from a watery sky
  That strikes at eve along some roaring beach,
  And tells the coast, from cliff to curving reach,
That light hath been, and is, and will not die;—
So flashed a revelation to her face,—
  Flashed and was gone; and, musing after her,
My heart still trembled like a woodland mere
  Wherein some goddess, pausing from the chase,
Hath dipped, and left its waters all astir
  To think what beauty ventured their embrace.

THE ASTRONOMER.

More worlds than one?
Who saith it is not so?
Have not I traversed to and fro
The astral sea, and wintered in the sun?

Have not I seen
The living thoughts of God
Work out their work, till men have trod
Where yesterday no solid earth had been?

Shall not I see,
(O shall I not, ere long!)
New meaning in the ecstatic song
Of morning stars, that, round their Father's knee,

Grow up to Him,—
Grow up to Him, and move
Through cycles waxing rich in love,
As day by day, from what was false and dim,

To clear and true
Their comprehension grows,—
To trust his purpose, as He knows
Their weakness, and his own delight to do?

A PHOTOGRAPH.

Daughter of Light,—of Light, and of that bride
   Whom unto Light the godlike mind hath brought,—
   Of Light and Earth, thy shape in darkness wrought,
Till on Earth's breast Light saw thee glorified ;
O through what pains, through what an envious tide
   Of perilous haps, all threatening to make nought
   Thy unconfirmed existence, hast thou sought
The life wherein thou shalt to time abide !
Lo ! now the star-led regents of my heart
   Approach thy footstool, offering unto thee
Their costliest gifts, for unto them thou art
   The counterfeit of that which sets them free
From all things base,—herself, in every part,
   Who through compassion hath redeeméd me.

THAWING.

A softer sky, a milder air,
    A few fine drops of rain;—
A softer word or glance from her
    Who hath my soul in chain.

A ramble through the forest ways
    To greet the snowdrop's eye;—
A reverie of coming days
    Too sweet for such as I.

O will the north wind turn again,
    And blight the darling flower?
O will the tender drops of rain
    Confess once more its power?

O will my lady, even yet,
    Her tenderness withdraw,
And leave my constancy to fret
    Round hers that will not thaw?

DEATH OR LIFE.

SAD dying woods, that take the last fond kiss
   Of sad November's last declining day,
   That from your height of vantage seem to say
" My friend departeth ; fain I would not miss
His latest speech,"—O tell me, what is this
   That holds my heart in bondage while I stray
     Round your dull skirts, this grief that seems to weigh
Like shadows of unutterable bliss ?
Is it the spirit's testament of woe,
   The plaint of hope that vainly seeks its lord ?
Or are they not like signs that come and go
Amid the surgings of a race brought low,—
   A race that soon, at one heart-stirring word,
   Shall rise and break their fetters with their sword ?

CONCLUSIONS.

Behold how Time prepares
Leagues of firm peace and bonds of brotherhood,
That bid the nations, satisfied with blood,
Beat spears to hooks, and swords to harmless shares;
    And yet is passion mightier than they.

Behold what arts of hell
War, passion's slave, industriously invents,
Bruising the force of hostile armaments
With chill steel shot, and horror-scattering shell;
    And yet is courage mightier than they.

Behold what endless pains
Are yearly spent to render clear and pure
The wells of being,—all disease to cure
That marks our social life with lep'rous stains;
    And yet is nature mightier than they.

Behold how cultures grow!
With what increased exactitude their wheels
Work each with each, until the learner feels
A dumb despair at what the learnéd know;
    And yet the soul is mightier than they.

O then, since life is short,
And leaves not time to fitly study all,
Hold to the greater, let the lesser fall
Unto their share with whom it doth consort,
    And know that thou art mightier than they.

ACCEPTED LOVE.

If but the touch of this exulting breeze,
   Warm from embracings with the flowering heath,
   That blows through all the twilight, from beneath
A pillar'd sky o'erhanging cold, gray seas,—
If but these sweets, and many such as these,
   Can draw the prisoned senses from their sheath,
   And build for them, across the waste of death,
A bridge that mounts through crowned eternities;—
O then reflect, cast up and count again,
   Through what starred reaches of infinity
I found myself uplifted from the plain
   Of life, that time I bent in trust the knee
Within the spirit's most inviolate fane,
   And through thy love God's answer breathed on me.

THE STEPMOTHER.

She walks with them by shelving shore,
    Along the beach, across the down,
Her heart the central heart to four
    That day by day draw near her own.

They walk with her, and think her kind,
    And in their childish conclaves say
They had not ever hoped to find
    A love like that which ebbed away.

Intent she studies every mood,
    And if her knowledge seems to fail
She sighs for her who understood
    Each heart like some familiar tale.

And daily as their pleased surprise
    Grows less before her boundless will,
They see not in the stranger's eyes
    Their mother's spirit watching still.

SILENT CHANGE.

Speeds Time more slowly in that as he speeds
   With noiseless touch he wears our lives away,
   And by the very slowness of decay
The soul with hopes of changeless being feeds?
Ah! not more slowly, o'er brine-scented weeds
   That fringe the banks of some storm-haunted bay,
   Creeps the flood tide, what though the tranquil day
Goes breathless down, and tranquil night succeeds.
Though winds are still, and skies no longer grand
   With stormy flashes of aërial war,
Yet on this sea-faced hillock take thy stand,
   And watch yon flat become a lessening bar,
Then melt away in threads and beads of sand,
   Till where it spread burns each reflected star.

"I SHALL BE SATISFIED."

When?   In that thrilling moment of decay,
  The last breath gone, the last pulsation ceased,
And what was man no more than potter's clay?
    Not then, not then.

When?   In that visioned advent from the east
  Of judgment, like an all-revealing day,
To prove our least the greatest, greatest least?
    Not then, not then.

When?   After million centuries of light
  Have cleansed the spirit, struggling still to burst
From life to life, as unto day from night?
    Not then, not then.

O glorious future! Morning never cursed
  With noon that faints and wearies!   To thy height
Climb upward still!   O God, we thirst, we thirst,
    Till then, till then!

SORROW.

Sorrow, dark night wherein true souls embrace
   Tenfold more closely than the gazing day
   Hath sufferance for, beneath whose mystic sway
Thoughts that may be the saviours of a race
From crude conception first begin to trace
   That outward shape which shall in time portray
   Their very features, who, when as it lay
In infant strength, most fondly watched its face ;—
Well dost thou deck thy canopy with stars,
   Portals of that most infinite abyss
Which joy shuts out with sure though golden bars,—
   Where dwell those solemn ecstasies of bliss
That burn away the soul's remaining scars
   When Death brings near his reconciling kiss.

A BIRTHDAY.

BEHIND the tops of yonder grove
    The east begins to burn ;
O birthday of my infant love,
    Hail to thy first return !

How dost thou dawn ? The pane is branched
    With childhood's crystal maze ;
Beneath pale stars the fields lie blanched;
    White drifts are in the ways.

How dost thou rise ? The southern heat
    With northern winds doth war,
And where the shadows cross the street
    Their shifting outposts are.

How dost thou fall ? A flaming crown,—
    A wheel of clouds and fire,
That centres o'er the westward down,
    And dies, an ash-strewn pyre.

ONE BLOSSOM.

As one who in a garden seeks delight,
   And, to his heartfelt sorrow, only finds
   The cruel wreck of unconsidering winds,
Or incompleteness of untimeous blight;
Till, suddenly, his unexpecting sight
   Is blest by some perfection, which unbinds
   All springs of worship, and all memory blinds
Save to that bloom so excellently bright;—
So, seeking beauty in the soul's great field,
   Grieved at what frosts had nipped or storms downtrod,
   I came where sure some kind enchanter's rod
Had worked a marvel; there perforce I kneeled
Chained where one soul's perfection shone revealed,
   Free, radiant, glorious in the light of God.

A CONJUNCTION.

In the chills of early dawn,
Night's deep mantle half withdrawn,
Shone Diana's curving bar
Close beside the morning star ;
Breathing from the vault above
Silvern chasteness, golden love.

Bright and brighter grew the east,
Day's white armies all released ;
Star-framed Titans, one by one,
Quenched their torches in the sun ;
Still that mystery shone above—
Silvern chasteness, golden love

O my love, whose dew-lit eyes
Watched at dawn the glimmering skies,
Watched, perchance, to trace some sign
Blessing that sweet life of thine,
Watched with all the faith and truth
Dwelling in the dreams of youth ;—

A CONJUNCTION.

O my love, what perfect thought,
Drenched with morning, star-inwrought,
Glorious with enchantment, stole
In that moment to thy soul,
Crowning with a golden light
Vague forelongings, angel-white?

Who shall guess and who shall say?
Yet, methinks, thy rising day,
When perchance it broadens soon
To the blaze of nuptial noon,
Still shall hold that sign above,—
Silvern chasteness, golden love.

WIDENING LIFE.

The simplest thoughts have beauty ; those which flow
   From the pure heart like water from a spring
   So far aloft that only by the wing
Of hovering eagles is the mid-day glow
Shut from its glancing pebbles ; thoughts which know
   Their value only by the tears they bring
   From simple eyes that love not anything
More than the splendour of the virgin snow.
Once was thy sunlit course such hills among ;
   Yet grieve thou not that now, O prospering soul,
Thy stream grows broad, and when the rains are long
   Begins through all the bordering woods to roll
A full majestic music, like the song
   Of coming power that knows but one control.

THE MOORLAND.

The moorland, O the moorland,
   The long-backed, lonely moor!
In light so warm, so cold in storm,
   So green, and yet so hoar;
So fierce and yet so gentle,
   So calm, and yet so wild,
The whole world's right, the soul's delight,
   The dream of every child.

The moorland, O the moorland,
   The airy, sunlit moor!
Where light and wind at daybreak twined
   The crown which sunrise wore;
Where cloudless noon sits silent,
   And where the evening cries,
All flaming gold, "Behold! behold!
   The plains of Paradise!"

THE MOORLAND.

The moorland, O the moorland,
    The mazy, moonlit moor !
Where whispers pass from heath to grass
    To dim the tarn's bright floor ;
Where climb and fall the Titans,
    While the slow Wain moves round,
Where facts are dreams, and stillness seems
    The perfectness of sound.

The moorland, O the moorland,
    The dismal, dreadful moor !
When downward beats the rain in sheets
    With gleam and blaze and roar ;
When torrent foams to torrent,
    And gloom replies to gloom,
And by the fires of torch-lit pyres
    The Summer seeks his tomb.

The moorland, O the moorland !
    O calm, enduring moor,
Thou hear'st the scream of headlong steam
    Thy secret depths explore ;
And all along the valleys
    Thou see'st the windows shine
Where toil and smoke man's slumber broke
    When God's sweet dawn broke thine.

THE MOORLAND.

The moorland, O the moorland !
   O lovely, lonely moor,
To thee still turns each heart that yearns
   To grasp what lies before ;
And all along the valleys
   Through smoke they cry to thee,
"Come weal or woe, come shine or snow,
   Yet give us liberty !"

A WAKEFUL NIGHT.

Whether the night wherein this wild uproar
   Of rain-drenched tempest holds mine eyes from sleep,
   Beholds thee waking also, fain to weep
For lack of rest thy spirit needeth more
Than do these eyelids ; whether thou dost pore,
   As I o'er books, over some thought more deep
   Than books contain, or bid'st thy fancies sweep
Into song's land unhelped by rhythmic oar,
I can but guess.   Yet this is certainty,—
   That all about thy life-long watch is drawn
A wall more firm than keeps this storm from me ;
   That in thy soul faith's flame, though oft assailed
Burns, as my lamp, unshaken, till 'tis paled
   By brighter splendour of the wished-for dawn.

THE SPRING.

No lower stoops the driving cloud
    When leaves are at their fall
Than where is seen against the green
    Yon white unquarried wall.

Nor higher mount the nutter's steps
    Upon the unshaded rise
Than where the pool, at noon still cool,
    Beneath the white cliff lies.

Thence drops anon the tiny rain,
    A mist that roams at will;
Thence feet anon go wandering on
    Upward and upward still.

Yet alway there the line is marked,
    As by some wayside inn,
Where ends the strife of actual life,
    And where its dreams begin.

THE SPRING.

O Spring, the fruit of heaven's pure love,
  That falls in falling showers,
Through what a maze of secret ways,
  Through what mysterious hours ;—

O Spring ! through what an age of pains
  Hath crept thy gurgling wave,
Before, so bright, it seeks the light
  From earth's forsaken grave !

Before, a crystal stream of life,
  It wells and wells for aye,
Too pure to hide the basin's side,
  Too glad to map the sky !

ELECTION.

In the world's visions I have seemed to see
   A house of mirth by revellers tenanted,
   To one of whom an entering herald said—
" This from thy Master,—straightway follow me ; "
And showed, in token of his dignity,
   A broken branch, whose earlier leaves were dead,
   But at whose tip fresh buds began to spread,
The promise of renewed vitality.
And then, methought, amid the scorn of those
   To whose unworthiness no hand should bring
A sign so rich in hope, that guest arose,
   And gladly with his guide went journeying,
Who led him forth by many a vale of woes,
   And crowned him in the wilderness a king.

"GRANT US THY PEACE."

The mountain murmured to the falling rain,
    The river to his banks, full high with flood,
The grass to the red lilies, and the grain
    To the sweet orchard's early blossoming bud;
" All things, O Lord, by quietude increase,—
        Grant us thy peace.

" All things, O Lord; yet man hath edged his blade,
    Hath charged with woe the sulphurous cannon's breath,
Unfurled his blood-stained battle-flag, and prayed
    Thy benediction on his fields of death;
Break thou his pride, bid thou his anger cease,—
        Grant us thy peace.

" O let the children lead again the lamb
    Through the still meads that bound the willowy brook;
No more alarms let clanging towers proclaim,
    Nor war-sounds fright the nestlings from their nook;
Give truce to tears, to prisoners release,—
        Grant us thy peace."

A JOURNEY.

Long hedgerows tipped with heraldings of Spring,
   Bright with the dews of morning ; then a stream,
   The salt highway by which large-minded steam
Goes forth upon his ocean journeying ;
And then for miles the busy, restless ring
   Of steel on steel, of wheels that alway seem
   To chafe at rest, suggesting many a dream
Of labour's ceaseless and resistless swing.
For miles on miles the dioramic show
   Of farm and wood, of stream and travelling sky,
Till, after noon, the light begins to grow
   Dull with the toil-born fogs that over-lie
The grand, sad heart of England, which we know
   Our journey's end and wished-for boundary.

"RUS IN URBE."

Her life was like a treeless town,
    That almost lives in doubt
If Spring still wears a flowery crown,
    If fields still lie without.

Her life was like a treeless town;
    Yet thither came at times
Some tender thought that was not grown
    In any soil of crimes.

That visioned forth the olden sweets
    Of stream or copse or sky,
Like violets sold in city streets
    When noon goes roaring by.

Like violets sold in city streets
    That set the noise and glare
In contrast with their green retreats,
    And ask "What do we here?"

HOPE.

THERE is a pleasure which is kin to pain,—
    Such pleasure as the faithful soul doth know
    When surging thought for some kind overflow
Doth strive and strive, yet striveth all in vain ;
When words return into their camps again,
    Scared from the assault, when even the fervid glow
    Of tear-filled eyes seems nothing, and the woe
Of owned shortcoming bids the lips refrain.
O happy Death, that in an hour so strange
    Dost seem the satisfaction of desire
Which finds no help within material range,—
    Shall not thy touch, when these faint flames expire,
    From their mute dust upraise a stronger fire,
Whose endless growth shall be its endless change ?

MAXWELL SQUARE (EAST LONDON).

THE trees are green in Maxwell Square,
    The trees are green with every Spring,
And rock their leaflets to the air
    That thitherward comes wandering
From fields and skies at all times sweet
Through stifling lane and stirring street.

The trees are green in Maxwell Square,
    And year by year they shed their leaves
To make a softer carpet where
    The children shout on Summer eves ;
And year by year the change goes on
Through which the world's great age hath gone.

The trees are green in Maxwell Square,—
    Are dull by night, are bright by day,
And nightly on them falls the glare
    Through restless doors across the way ;
Through doors that ope and close again
Like Summer lightning on the main.

MAXWELL SQUARE (EAST LONDON).

The trees are green in Maxwell Square,—
   They live their life from Spring to Spring,
And have no thought that all things there—
   The babes that shout, the doors that swing,
The streets beneath, the fumes above—
Are aught but revelries of love.

O trees so green in Maxwell Square,
   Could ye but gauge the tide that flows
About your stems,—how all unfair
   Each childish life, how black with woes
The flashing doors where guilt goes in
To find a Lethe for its sin ;—

O trees too green in Maxwell Square,
   Would then your leaves be green no more,
But wither up in black despair
   To see the life that goes before—
The life that stands above your own—
So wrecked, so wrested, overthrown ?

O trees still green in Maxwell Square,
   We know not that, but this we know,—
That in the soul a sense of fair
   Makes aught unfair the fount of woe ;
That in the sharpest whips of crime
Gleam dawnings of the happier time.

HIGH DOWN, FRESHWATER.

Is there no voice in yonder cloud that draws
    Its miles of shadow over miles of sea?
    Or was that mount in thankless Galilee,
Or that which shook to thunder-breathèd laws,
The only spot where God's eternal cause
    Drew strength from more than man's weak agency,
    And flushed the streams of far-off history
With solemn thought which still inspires and awes?
Lo! even now yon headland waxes dim
    With clouds that stoop beneath the dreadful feet,
Beneath the noiseless chariot wheels of Him
    Who passes by; across the sunshine meet
The outstretched wings of lauding Cherubim,
    And the hushed waves with awe-struck pulses beat.

REMEMBRANCE.

Over where my love lies sleeping
   Constant still a flame is burning,
I, whom Time would wean from weeping,
   Find it year by year returning.

Then my heart its youth remembers,
   Then renews the pains of dying,
Blows a flame from fragrant embers,
   Tastes the wondrous sweets of sighing.

Lo! as sleep by night the roses
   'Mid the scents themselves were spreading,
Thus thy life, my love, reposes,
   Lapped in sweets it erst was shedding.

INDEPENDENCE.

"Put not thy trust in princes,"—even so ;
    Whether their smile continue alway kind,
    Or whether, treacherous as the southern wind
That brings a storm while lifting off the snow,
Their favour turn,—yet trust them not, e'en though
    They wield that higher sovereignty of mind,
    As if their greatness left not where to find
A throne more firm, their "yes" a mightier "no."
For time, that gives men sceptres, takes away,
    Oft in that giving, somewhat from the worth
Which led them up the long and perilous way
    Of lonely self-advancement ; on the earth
'Tis best to live with those who shall one day
    Be kings elected, not with kings by birth.

BY THE ESK.

O Esk, so swift, so brown, so clear,
    The latest of my friends art thou ;
And yet thy voice is far more dear
    Than many a voice well known ere now.

O somewhere 'mid thy woodland dells,
    In dreams, in ramblings of the night,
Or in some hope that oft foretells
    The slow fulfilment of delight ;—

O somewhere there, I know not when,
    My soul hath wandered oft and far,
At noon, or when thy shadowy glen
    Looked upward to the evening star.

I know the hazel's quivering copse,
    I know the wharf of foot-worn stone,
The silent pines, the tall oak tops,
    The sunlit scarp's majestic throne.

The lingering light that steals and shifts
    From reach to reach, from tree to tree,
The damp repose of ferny rifts,
    The willowed isle, are known to me.

And known to me the moss-grown weir,
    And known to me the pool, whose tide
Scarce creeps, conservative in fear,
    To tempt the rapid's dangerous slide.

O Esk, I know not what thou art ;
    I know not if indeed there goes
A winding current through my heart
    That linked with all thy winding flows.

Or if the force that slowly rent
    Thy widening passage to the sea
Hath somewhere worked its fateful bent
    On passive faults that slept in me.

"BLESSED ARE THE PEACE-MAKERS."

Not only they who to the petty feud
   Bring termination and consent to peace,
   Nor they who by their influence bid cease
The cannon's boom and echoing war-trump rude ;
Nor even they who heedfully exclude
   Mistrusts of nations, which, if let increase,
   Would the fierce war-dogs speedily release,—
Not to these only the beautitude
Of peace-makers pertains. But even more
   To those who, subtly conscious of the breath
Of coming changes, labour to restore
   The rock-hewn reservoirs of social faith ;
Who to men faltering open wide the door
   Through which new life beats down their dreams of death.

GOD-SPEED.

Go, faithful soul, the world's control
   No more shall vex thy will;
Sublime in life, this final strife
   Beholds thee victor still.
What though thy light departs our sight,
   Though yet we mourn thee gone,
Thy deeds remain, a glorious train,
   In splendour marching on.

Ah! faithful heart, our tears upstart,
   While up thy path we gaze;
Yet not for pain that gathering rain,
   'Tis joy too deep for praise.
In sun nor star thy pulses are,
   Thy mystery who can tell?
Yet somewhere near thy voice we hear,—
   We will not say "farewell."

WHITSUNTIDE.

No rushing wind, no hint of aught but calm
    Beneath the dome of this pure southern day,—
    The blue that wraps the hill-tops far away,
Yet seems innate in cool-winged breaths of balm
That hedge each movement, while, one silent psalm,
    The whole earth gazes upward, even as they
    Of Galilee once gazed, as if to stay
Him whom they fain, with popular shout and palm,
Had seen crowned victor. Yet if not all vain
    That upward gaze (as men have said) to draw
Some rich fulfilment down in fiery rain ;
So now, perchance, like dews upon the plain,
    Drop down those fruits which earlier minds foresaw,—
    Love, Joy, Hope, Peace, against which is no law.

VOX POPULI.

How long, how long upon that awful tree
    Wilt Thou yet hang? how long thy silent woe
Scare from the crest of feet-worn Calvary
    All gleams of light, all winds that come and go?
How long thy brow possess the thorny crown?
        If Thou be'st He, come down.

Where is the crowd that watched thy steps of pain
    Up that sad slope where still thy anguish dwells?
That hoped in Thee to see their paths made plain,
    Through Thee to bind each passion that rebels
Against that one eternity of love
        To which they feel they move?

They smote their breasts; perplexed, they hid their
    eyes;
    And all confounded each one went his way,
Some to their farms and some their merchandise,
    Leaving but one beneath the cross to pray;
Only one, outcast from the homes of men,—
        Only the Magdalen.

The grave gives up, the sea gives up its dead,—
   Truths dead to men that only lived in God ;
And, strangely tired, those self-same streets they tread
   Which, living, oft thy welcome footsteps trod.
Behold ! they wait for judgment ; wert not Thou
       Proclaimed their judge ere now ?

Behold ! we live ; we add with every breath
   Some scanty portion to the rising wall,
But thou dost linger in perpetual death
   Whom we would make the corner stone of all.
Shall God himself uncrown his labour thus ?
       Come down, and live with us.

YOUTH IN AGE.

To feel the waste of life, yet not to feel
   A loss of care for life's infinity,
   To see the grave, yet not therein to see
The dust of all that bear's true wisdom's seal ;
To mark new parliaments of thought repeal
   Much that the old had loudly held to be
   Man's final law, yet cry not " Blasphemy ! "
Nor bid God's judgment haste its tarrying wheel ;—
Lo ! thus to live is my most firm desire,—
   To think the world young, though the life wax old ;
And not like one that tends a wasting fire,
   Who, vexed with watching, ceaseth to uphold
The flame that seems just flickering to expire,
   And saith, " Sleep waits me ; let the earth be cold."

VOX DEI.

Who art thou wandering on a midnight sea,
    Who all at once art frighted and dismayed
To watch one walking o'er the waves to thee,—
    A soul accursed from rest, a ghost unlaid?
Hear thou the voice that calleth in reply,—
The well-known voice that answers, "It is I,—
      "Be not afraid."

Who art thou fainting 'mid the fevered wild
    Of burning thoughts, who loudly dost upbraid
The fierce desire that called thee when a child,
    And led thee hither, far from kindly aid?
Lo! 'twas my hand which strongly grasped thine own!
And shall I leave thee perishing alone?
      Be not afraid!

Who art thou turning backward from the morn
    That shows the rock whereon thy trust was stayed
A tottering fragment, weather-marked and torn,
    Gaping with rifts which Time's great waves have made?
Yet 'twas my word that raised that ponderous wall;
Yet 'tis my word that bids its remnant fall;—
      Be not afraid.

WINTER IN THE SOUTH.

ALL yesterday the strong sirocco blew,
    And evening fell with thunder-threatening gloom;
    Breathless at last, and silent as the tomb,
The day went out in darkness; only through
One solemn rift Orion's belt up-drew
    The soul to ask what prodigy of doom
    Thus slept encurtained. Then from out the womb
Of midnight stole, whence gendered no man knew,
A clear, soft coolness; then the roofs with rain
    All gently echoed, while the dust, washed down
From flower and leaf, lay moistened in the lane;
    Till, through a thousand breezy openings blown,
The pure white morning benison'd the plain,
    And life and hope retwined their floral crown.

THE MADONNA.

Crowned with the worship of a thousand years,
Robed with the glory of a godlike name,
    Thy face all light, thine eyes all tears,—
    Tears which thy human heart proclaim,
Light which declares thy certain right to be
        Man's chief divinity :—

Light, not of tapers kindled on the shrine
Where, through the rolling depths of incense clouds,
    Thy pictured countenance divine
    Looks forth upon the kneeling crowds,
Moving each soul with whispers of that love
        Which fills thy world above :—

But light of good performèd for thy sake,
Of evil at thy bidding left undone,
    Of unrecorded deeds that make
    The earth less dark beneath the sun,
Of many vows and countless words of prayer,
        Confessing thy sweet care :—

Crowned with such worship, with such light o'er-
    spread,
In visioned trance I see thee slowly rise,
    As when before the uncurtained bed
    Of him whose pencil from the skies
Drew all its fire, thy radiant image stood
        In virgin matronhood.

Thy smile is toward the burthen of thine arms,
Whose glance sheds forth so unrestrained a peace
    That all the vague unblest alarms
    Of judgment trumpets straightway cease,
And dead things wake to swell the moving host
        Of love that counts not cost.

Mother of Life,—for thou didst bring forth Him
Who was and is the one true Life of men,—
    Shall all thine altar lights grow dim?
    Or shall the years restore again
That faded faith that brought the world to thee
        In gladsome unity?

Are there no tears left in this world of ours?
Are there no weak still trampled by the strong?
    Is there no need for mercy's showers
    O'er wastes of self-avenging wrong?
Is there no love that clasps for its reward
        The piercing of the sword?

Lo ! these things are ; and over them thy smile,—
The smile of wisdom chastened by deep pain,—
    Shines like a taper through the aisle
    Whose shadows drink the last refrain
When thy great psalm of benediction rolls
        Through thousand quivering souls.

Until no harvest of enduring hearts
The ploughed and broken generations bear,
    Thy glory fades not nor departs,
    Nor cease those incense clouds of prayer
That call thee, as thyself proclaimed of yore,
        Blessèd for evermore.

PATIENT WORK.

The years slip by, and youth, that fain had woo'd
    Our lives to bright and perilous intents,
    Outlives itself; as the wild steed consents
To brook the bridle, so, with pace subdued,
We soberly step forward, while a mood
    Of self-suspicion haunts us, nor relents,
    Asking, "Is this to high heroic bents
" The only fruit of action ?   Is the good
" As year by year the pulse more slowly beats,
    "Less valued?" Nay ; for those who ponder well
Life's inner mystery, count youth's passionate heats
    Less worthy than the staid desires that dwell
With souls made pure by merciful defeats,
    And that, through waiting, patiently excel.

ONLY.

Can this be only sky?
   This field of flaming gold,—
   Of crimson fold on fold
In regal majesty?

Can this be only sea?
   This plain so wide and dim,
   Far-stretching to the rim
Where day doth cease to be?

Can these be only sails
   That from the sunset come
   Like ghosts, to seek a home
At rest from sea-born gales?

Begone, blaspheming word!
   "Only"—the soul begins
   A year all black with sins
When once thy sound is heard.

9

ONLY.

O if with seas or skies,
    Or labouring ship that brings
    On avarice-tainted wings
The dust of merchandise ;—

If aught of birth more rare
    Appear to dwell with these,
    Think what the spirit sees
Alone existeth there.

MUTUAL HELP.

Even as ships that on the midway deep
    By interchange of fluttering signals find
    The self-same port awaits them, and though wind,
Unspringing swiftly in the hours of sleep,
Parts them by wide horizons, nathless keep
    Each other's progress constantly in mind—
    Well wotting of the steadfast stars that bind
Their paths together—till at last they sweep
Into their haven;—even so with souls
    That, met by chance, each unto each make known
Their joint obedience to the same controls;
And live thenceforward, though between them rolls
    Circumstance like a sea, not twain, but one—
    Apart, not parted—lonely, yet not lone.

THE LAST HOPE.

"Man doth not live by bread alone,"—
    Say then, O prophet, how lives he?
When joys are dashed and hopes are gone
    What else but bread his food can be?

What other lot can then be his
    Save this—to live the sensual round
From day to day, and think it bliss
    Whenever sleep his eyes hath found?

"Man doth not live by bread alone,"—
    O prophet, say'st thou not a lie?
For even bread thus turned to stone
    Can only give him strength to die.

Yet there is something even then,
    O man, by which thy soul may live,—
The deep regret that holds thee when
    Earth hath no bread but stones to give.

SILENT INFLUENCE.

METHOUGHT I saw before some judgment throne—
  Whether in earth or heaven I might not tell—
  A soul from whose sad lips this utterance fell,—
"Lo! I am naught: what good thing have I done?"
Then came this word in answer—"Is there none
  "To plead herein?" And straightway like the swell
  Of organ-breathèd symphonies that dwell
In high church roofs, came echoing back the tone
Of countless voices;—"I, and I, and I!
  "Clear through the darkness shone thy heaven-fixed will,
  "And we that, unseen, saw it, lived thereby!"
They ceased; and lo! as some high-towering hill
Flames in the sunrise, so, with hands raised high,
  Amazed at its own worth, that soul stood still.

"WE MIGHT."

No cypress boughs that wail and wave
    Can spread so deep a night
Above the exile's nameless grave
    As these two words, " We might."

We might have borne, we might have strove
    To see the good that grew
Beneath the fault, and bent our love
    To aid its bursting through.

We might have felt his burning pain,
    Nor sent him to despair
In haste that we might breathe again
    The world's serener air.

We might have pierced beneath the scorn
    With which he cried, "I go!"
And seen his life destroyed and torn
    With all-despairing woe.

We might have kept the curse unknown
   To see him evermore
Appeal against us to the throne
   Whose love self-love forswore.

O solemn tense that takes our ease
   In pledge for old mistrust !
O most supreme of God's decrees,—
   " We may—we might—we must."

THE MAGDALEN.

"Wherever," said the Master, "shall be told
    "My story, there shall likewise be proclaimed
    "That which this woman, whom your frowns
        have blamed,
"Hath done to me before you." And behold!
The action lives, a truth of purest gold
    From which the sceptic's acid turns ashamed,—
    An action alway with emotion named,
As touching thoughts which never can grow old.
No chance was this; for as through starry space
    The ladder of man's light is lifted higher
From posts more wide apart, so face to face
    When suffering guilt met suffering love, a fire
Flashed forth to point the future of a race
    Through dim-lit gulfs of fathomless desire.

EVENING.

O LIGHT that knows not end or space,
    O day that knows not fall or rise,
Thy glory shines upon my face
    E'en while this fleeting daylight dies.

O sun supreme in central might,
    Whose orb the widest orbit knows,
To thee from these sweet gates of night
    My soul in rapture overflows.

As noontide wraps the world in light
    So let thy truth be mine alway,
And let me move from right to right,
    As day succeeds again to day.

O light that knows not space nor end,
    O day that knows not rise or fall,
From strength to strength our souls ascend,
    And find thee still their all in all.

HOLY GROUND.

FRESH from the touch of irritating cares—
    Those envious thorns with which our road is twined—
    From strifes that soil, and harassments that blind
To life's sublimer meaning, unawares,
As on a garden fenced and free from tares,
    I chanced upon the pathways of a mind
    Where sprung, well tended, growths of every kind
Which, unembittered, later girlhood bears.
Not much, perchance; but certes there were found
    Patience self-schooled and high Sincerity,
While Love and Hope contentedly sat crowned
    With gentle thoughts. Straightway there breathed to me
    A still small whisper:—" These, then, dost thou see?
" Put off thy shoes,—this spot is holy ground!"

PARTED.

Whene'er the night, long waited for, returning,
  Brings to my heart an all too brief repose,
Ah! then with what unfathomable yearning,
  Friend of my earlier victories and woes,
     "Appear, appear!" I cry to thee,
     "Though but a wandering shade thou be!"

Lo! from yon star methinks a voice is speaking;
  "Know'st thou me not, beloved?" it seems to say;
"Here am I nightly present to thy seeking,
  Here wait a little forward on thy way."
     "O, if 'tis thou," my lips reply,
     "Burn till the morning floods the sky!"

Faint, faint my speech, and fainter thy replying—
  A silver wave scarce moved across the deep;
Like parted streams unto each other sighing,
  Like a faint chant that rocks itself to sleep;
     Now doubted of, now heard, now mute,
     Like wind-struck music from the lute.

Ah! dost thou ask, not mindless of my sorrow,
  Ah ! dost thou ask, if tears are now my lot,
May there not come, perchance, a tearless morrow,
  When thou, with all the past, shalt be forgot?
    Ah ! sooner thus than reap thy blame
     Each hour that strikes shall sound thy name !

THE LAST MARTYR.

("FATHER DAMIEN has died of leprosy at Molokai, in the Sandwich Islands."—*Reuter's Telegram.*)

"WHO for us men"—so runs the chanted creed—
   " And for our saving once from heaven came down,"
   Claiming thereby the kingdom and the crown
Of earth and worlds celestial. Who such deed
Could work save God himself? So preachers plead,
   While year by year the dust of history, thrown
   On warm tradition, blots it, till the known
Seems like some island further to recede
'Mid seas of doubt. When lo! 'tis advertised
   That one hath died who for life's genial smile
Exchanged the blackest doom by death devised,
   If but a brother's woes he might beguile.
No God, but man; and men, to tears surprised,
   Find a new Calvary in that reef-girt isle.

WHICH?

Soul to soul and heart to heart,
Loving still, yet held apart,
Touching daily hands with hands,
Yet as if in alien lands;
Tell me, darling, tell me this,—
Is it torture—is it bliss?

Is it joy, forsooth, to gain
Glimpses of each other's pain?
In this all unfruitful state
Owe we gratitude to fate,—
Fate that o'er the bitter wall
Suffers us to speak at all?

Is it torture, love, to know
That our souls, for weal or woe,
Linked by hidden chains advance
Through the wastes of time and chance?
Were the truth beyond our guess,
Would the sting of life be less?

WHICH?

Be it torture, be it bliss,
In the gloom our spirits kiss;
Kiss like lovers that, forlorn,
Dread the farewells of the morn;
Dread—yet hope—yet dare not pray
For the certain light of day.

ADOPTION.

O EARTH! Earth! Earth! with many an age of throes
  Hast thou brought forth into the world of light
  Spirits whom aye their Father doth invite
To dwell with Him, and have their lot with those
Whom, passed beyond the need of cleansing woes,
  He leads with joy from height to vaster height,
  Opening new deeps of glory infinite
Unto their sight that ever grows and grows.
O Earth! would'st thou reclaim them? would'st thou gall
  With bondage those enfranchised lives again,
Which even aforetime scarce thou could'st enthrall?
  Are they thine offspring? Yea, but there are twain
That call them sons; and if their Father call
  Will not thy cry be uttered forth in vain?

TWILIGHT.

When the day is almost done,
When the glare and noise are gone,
Comes at last a dream of rest,
Whispered from the glimmering west;
Comes at last a dream of care,
Lulled to sleep by Lydian air,
Dream of conquest for the brave,—
Sleep for warrior, sleep for slave.

From the gates of night is borne
Incense as of April morn;
Life, reviving, wakes again
On the verge of death's domain;
Thoughts that wandered in the past
Find, surprised, a home at last
In the chastened hope that steals
Round to dawn on golden wheels.

FORECASTING.

As I have seen a mother softly bend
   Above the cot wherein her babe doth lie,
   That straightway smiled, while yet unclosed its eye,
As if it felt the nearness of a friend,—
As if it felt an influence descend
   That raised it up from thoughtless infancy,
   And gave it glimpses of a wider sky
Which it recalls not, nor can comprehend;—
So in these veiled existences of ours,
   Which are but sleep, whose thoughts are infants'
      dreams,
We are o'erwatched, maybe, by larger powers,
   That bend above us in some hope that seems
The visioned crown of all aspiring hours,—
   The large clear lake that feedeth all our streams.

A SONG OF SOLWAY.

O'er Solway's worn and watery shore
    The trailing fogbank flies;
But damper far these eyelids are
    With tears that needs must rise.

The wave is white on Solway's breast
    And bitter blows the wind;
But far more white my lips to-night,
    And far more tossed my mind.

O Mary, lost through envious fate,
    O now thy form I see
Upon the sand with help-stretched hand;
    But can thy soul see me?

O was it more than watery wave,
    And more than failing breath
That parted me that day from thee?
    Hath life itself no death?

O when I look upon the past
   I seem to stand alone
Upon a shore that more and more
   Recedeth from thine own.

I see once more the wet mists fly
   As on that night they flew;
The salt waves flow, the hoarse winds blow
   As on that night they blew.

And more and more the waters rise,
   And closer creep around;
The last dim cape receives thy shape,
   And I myself am drowned.

HELP.

Ah! is it then a strange, unbalanced thought
   That those who passed before us on the road
   By which we travel, under such a load
As bids us ask if all our toil be naught,—
Seems it so strange, so far removed from aught
   The mind should welcome, that, in many a node
   Of chance and will, the exit thence is showed
By help of some through like experience taught?
Lo! from the misty step on which I stand,
   So near the foot of Truth's eternal stair,
I, even I, may love to stretch a hand
   In help to some beneath; and should this care,
Born in the ascent to what is pure and grand,
   Grow less and less as these grow large and fair?

THE VIOLIN-PLAYER.

O long-drawn sigh !
Born in the looking back
Of Orpheus on the vacant track,
How dost thou swell, how ghost-like dost thou die !

O sparkling wave !
Art thou not from the beach
Whose sand is gold from reach to reach,
Where Tritons sport, and sea-nymphs haunt the cave ?

O solemn tone !
Dissolving earthly bars,
Leading the soul triumphant to the stars,
Where crowned it sits, and speaks with thee alone !

O vast accord !
O grief ! O sea ! O sky !
What thing is man, whose harmony
Thus seeks thee out, and makes itself thy lord ?

EARLY VISIONS.

WHERE are they then, the wise, the pure, the true,—
   God's great invisible teachers, where are they?
   Is't all in vain to scan the arch of day,
Or pierce the night's unfathomable blue?
Is there no voice that speaks, no transient view
   Of wingless forms that tread some airy way,
   Are there no hosts whose unforeseen array
Can bid us yet our drooping trust renew?
Were these things once? Yet are they all withdrawn
   Into that cavernous limbo of the past
Which for the present ceaseth not to yawn;
   Were these things once, yet scarcely could they last
   Beyond the clouds on which their shapes were cast,—
Beyond the age of manhood's misty dawn.

A STATUE.

Silent, whatever else may stir,
   And sweet, whatever else seem rude,
In thy cold life recalling her
   Whom warm the world at no time viewed ;—

So sweetly evermore be dumb,
   So evermore be mutely sweet,
And to the wondering sense become
   A point where faith and sight may meet.

Thou hast no beauty, for thou art
   From where confusion looks not in;
Thou hast no virtue, for thy heart
   Hath not so much as heard of sin.

No dread of murderous lust is thine,
   No hope of sacrificing love,
Nor aught of what we call divine,
   Because, like cloud, it floats above.

But all in all thou dost reveal
    A life that moves beyond our ken,
So strange that whosoe'er doth feel
    For means to bind it nearer men,—

Stands shamed the while his labour flies
    To fragments, wasting all his pain;
Shattered as thy reflection lies
    Beneath the fountain's murmuring rain.

PROTECTION.

THAT some have talked with angels seemeth not
   So strange a thing as it had seemed to me
   If from the page of infant history
There looked forth no such legend, if no spot
Had been to some, whose inward strife was hot,
   The meeting-place with such a company
   As Jacob met, that time he feared to see
The face of him whose wrath pursued his lot
With long-nursed vengeance. For, considering well
   Amid what floods is based the rising tower
Of social being, hard it were to tell
   How toiled its founders on from hour to hour,
Despairing not, except they seemed to dwell
   In friendly league with supernatural power.

A DIALOGUE.

My crown is gemmed with million stars,
    And sheaves of bright blue days ;
Music that calms and hope-born palms,—
    A crown of shining rays.

My crown is dark with million woes,
    And black unfruitful morns ;
With doubt that fears and sin-born tears,—
    A very crown of thorns.

Along the free unboundaried height
    That overlooks the sea,
I watch the light proceed from night,
    And feel its joy through me.

Along the alley's dismal length,
    Where scarce a sunbeam falls,
I hear the song of shameless wrong
    Affright the tottering walls.

Yet sometimes 'mid triumphant notes
  I hear a different strain,
An echo cast from joys long past,
  That seems akin to pain.

And oft when sorrows crowd so thick
  That all lament is dumb,
There floats to me what seems to be
  A dream of joys to come.

HISTORY.

Yea, let the page of sacred history keep,—
   History, all sacred, in that it records
   The pangs of progress, in that it affords
A line to sound the farthest human deep,—
Let it retain (though wronged exactness weep,
   And claim the close imprisonment of words
   In narrow cells of meaning), all that hoards
Those inner faiths which far too often sleep.
Yea, let the comet usher in its train
   Sickness and famine ; let the unwonted star
Foretell Truth's advent ; let the arousing main
   Roll out its joy, beholding from afar
   The great adjustment, like a judgment bar,
Lightening the east, and quickening all the slain.

AN ANNIVERSARY.

Smilest thou, love ? 'Twas yesterday,
  One year ago, that first thy smile
Dropped down on my laborious way
  To dock the length of many a mile.

Smilest thou, love ? Ah ! yet to-day
  Thy smile retains its olden power ;
I feel no heat and fear no fray,
  And life is all one golden hour.

Smilest thou, love ? Ah ! not to-day,
  Nor yet to-morrow snaps the chain
That found us as we went astray,
  And made one path suffice for twain.

For when a million years are run,
  And when the earth we love so well
Hath not a name beneath the sun,
  The sun himself a worn-out shell ;—

Still shall thy soul's transcendent face
    Reflect the love that looks from mine,
As evermore we climb through space
    From more divine to more divine.

LOVE AND SORROW.

I DREAMED that Love and Sorrow chanced to meet
  Within a court where countless altars blazed
  Up to the stars whose unseen King they praised,—
Sorrow thorn-crowned, and Love whose light-winged feet
Burn in their haste their journey's end to greet;—
  That there they met, and on each other gazed
  With deep-set wonder, silently amazed
That from the other neither made retreat.
Till Love spake first:—" My name indeed is Love,
  And yet no bride is found on earth for me;
Will thou be mine?" And Sorrow looked above
  And saw the stars grow brighter. "It shall bé,"
She softly said; then, like a wearied dove,
  Drooped on his breast from whom she thought to flee.

LOVE'S TEMPLE.

Smoothness and softness and whiteness and warmth
  Sleep in thy bosom, my lady, my dear;
Smoothness and softness and whiteness and warmth,
  Dreamed of when absent and dreamed on when near.

Warm as the west wind that brings in the evening
  Light to the meadow whose wildflowers are wet,
Light like a dream in whose depths are entwining
  The last threads of hope with the first of regret.

White as the snow-drift that daintily covers
  All the dead sweets of the vanishing year,
All the new births that in secret are spreading
  Forth their faint hands to the spring drawing near.

Soft as the mercy that gently o'ershadows
  Life with its fierceness of triumph and pain,
Smooth as the passage of golden-winged hours
  Ebbing unfelt from the years that remain.

O temple of wonder, where mercy is dwelling,
   Where hope blends its tears with the sweets of regret,
Where sleep the faint mysteries of birth and of being,
   Where care leaves its burden and learns to forget;—

O temple of wonder, still throng to thy portal
   The children of labour for solace and peace,
And love is eternal and life is immortal
   Till with thee the earth and the heavens shall cease!

POETRY.

Scarce with the calmness of considerate age
    Dwells the poetic fervour, scarce with those
    Who from without take count of human woes,
As men take count of actors on the stage ;
Whose passion liveth only on the page
    That wots not whether agonising throes
    Of faith half-slain its chequered impress shows,
Or calm of hope, or love's despairing rage.
Scarce thus is passion mastered, from without ;
    Rather the man in whom its mastery dwells,
Whose faith is more than faith, whose doubt than doubt,
    Him oft a sudden ecstasy impels
Into the waste that compasses about
    The citied world ; and what he is, he tells.

AN ORACLE.

The wind's warm lips were pressed to mine
    As westward still I bore;
The wind's warm lips, all moist with brine
    From some foam-girdled shore.

O wind, so strong, so fresh, so free,
    Say, as thy gusts sweep by,
Is onward still the course for me
    Against yon threatening sky?

Must still the sunset and the main,
    Whose marge divides the night,
Whose breast is gray with gathering rain,
    Or streaked with doubtful light;—

Must still the sunset and the sea,
    The lone, unbeaten track,
My portion be, or is to me
    Thy word "Turn back, turn back!"

A murmur breathed around my ear
    As westward still I strove;—
"Shall doubt by those be seen as fear
    Who meet the lips they love?"

A HOLIDAY.

One clear glad day,—the happy laugh of girls,
    The outdoor lounge, the fixed yet changing view
    ' Across the fields, the town, the ships, the blue
Of Ind's far ocean, all its sand-locked swirls
Flashing with golden Aphroditè's curls,
    While over head the golden fruit burns through
    Dark foliage moving to the breeze that flew
At dawn to canvas which the eve upfurls
Above the fresh-dropped anchor. Such a day,
    Snatched from the turmoil of an anxious war,
Falls like some blest oäsis on the way
    Of sun-worn wanderers,—like the rock-perched star,
    That whispers to the sailor,—" Safe thus far,
Bear on till gleams the next directing ray."

PROTHALAMIUM.

Where is the hall which their bridal shall enter
   Whose rose hath been gathered both open and
      whole?
Blushing its petals and burning its centre,
   Yearning of body and passion of soul?

Never for us be the pride of the palace,
   Where gold gleams around us and marble above;
Never that poison corrupting the chalice,—
   Luxury, soulless, laughing at love!

Far from the tumult of turbulent cities,
   Far from the streets by prosperity trod,
Far from the portals where insolence pities
   Poverty robed in the likeness of God;—

Far let us fly to some verge of the ocean,
   Where the deep shadow of murmuring trees
Bends with a kiss to the indolent motion
   Swelling unmeasured o'er fathomless seas.

PROTHALAMIUM.

Thither, O bride of a million desires,
   Thither thy footsteps at evening shall come,
While the first star, with its silvery fires,
   Burns like Love's torch in the deepening dome.

There shalt thou rest 'mid the fragrance of flowers,
   Lave thy pure feet in the curls of the stream,
Watching in silence while maidenhood's hours
   Break into joy from the depths of their dream.

Then, when the rosy-hued twilight that saw me
   Steal to thy shelter, just lingering, dies,
Clasp thy soft arms round my neck, love, and draw me
   Down to thy lips by the soul in thine eyes.

JUDGE NOT.

Safe as thou art in passion's temperate zone,
    Thy wildest thoughts pulsating calmly by
    Ordered by custom, proud that they defy
No trivial law, of climes unlike thine own
How canst thou judge? By what to thee is known
    How gauge the force of storms, that, o'er a sky
    Of tenfold brightness, shake forth suddenly
Death's ensign, and beneath it rule alone?
Reward thou hast, and keep it; yet who knows
    (Yea, who knows not?) but what the silent pain,
Scourging transgression in the hearts of those
    Who, without rule, live out their lives, nor rein
One generous impulse, more divineness shows
    Than all thy abstinent virtues can attain?

INCONSTANCY.

One moon for him, and one for me,
    Two for thyself, and all for love,—
When will thy planet cease to be
    Begirt like that of watery Jove?

One moon for me and one for him,—
    His lights the east ere mine is gone,
And ere his moon is waxing dim,
    Conjoint, thy twain come marching on.

O lives there not some wished-for night,
    Some night much blessed with prosperous stars,
When thine not risen, and his from sight
    Beyond the sunset's reddening bars;—

When mine alone, full-orbed and clear,
    Shall kiss the east, shall rise and rise
From amber to the silvery sphere,—
    Sole regnant of the adoring skies?

A REVELATION.

Weeping for weakness? Nay, I wept for strength;
   As one who venturously the rock hath scaled,
   With foot that trembled not, nor hand that failed,
Till on the brow he lays him down at length;
And then the life that for a space before
   Had held a silent conference with death,
   Comes swelling back in waves that choke the breath,
While every heart-throb cries, "I live once more!"
So, scaling long a precipice of thought,
   Grasping at "ifs" that, grasped at, half gave way,
I touched at last an act which one had wrought
   Not knowing wherefore. Into me it rushed
"This is the sunshine, this the clear bright day!"
   And through my tears hope's morning shone new flushed.

LIVINGSTONE.

If, dying in a lonely land,
  Remote from friendship, void of ease,—
Dying when sparkled close at hand
  The last home passage o'er the seas ;—

Dying when all the world was rife
  With growing whispers of his praise,
The victor in a self-sought strife,
  The self-sustained in lonely ways ;—

If dying thus, there still should be
  Some lips to murmur, " It is well,—
'Tis well for soldiers such as he
  To rest in honour where they fell ;—

" 'Tis well that memory needs must fly
  The funeral psalm, the gothic vault,
To seek beneath a tropic sky
  The fevered traveller's final halt ;—

" 'Tis well, 'tis better thus for him
    To sanctify the soil he trod,
To feel, when sights and sounds grew dim,
    His spirit face to face with God ;—

" 'Tis better that, to those who wait
    To crown with laurels his return,
The soul should come, through death more great,
    And not the body, frail and worn : "—

If thus, maybe some wider glance
    Than wisest thought can entertain,
That scans the tangled threads of chance,
    And sees in loss a deeper gain ;—

Maybe such glance as this doth mark
    Where souls, by fortune over-wrought,
Tread in the loneliness and dark
    Unkindly wastes of life and thought ;—

Beholds them setting forth at first,
    Too blindly brave to need a friend,
Drawn onward by their quenchless thirst
    To trace their problem to the end ;—

Beholds them when at last they sink,
    Still friendless, hopeless, on the plain,
Slain more than all by this—to think
    That all has been endured in vain ;—

Beholds them with a smile whose light
   Sheds on them through life's lifting veil
The truth that those who nobly fight
   Are victors even when they fail.

RESPONSIBILITY.

If after all our life were but a dream,
   A swarm of cloudy unrealities
   That sink to nothing even as they rise,
As sinks the ripple on the travelling stream ;
If guilt's despair and outraged honour's scream,
   The froth of fools, the empire of the wise,
   All that men value, all that they despise,
Were nought but names, things which are not, but seem ;
Then might indeed the wordy tournament,
   The ghostly clash of philosophic swords,
The unremitting labour to invent
   New schemes for earth, new kindred for its lords,—
Then might such tasks consume a life well spent ;
   But acts are acts, for all the smoke of words.

DIRGE.

Waking late and rising early,
    Lengthening out the toils of day,
One thought only, shining clearly,
    Sheds its radiance on my way ;
'Mid the city's ceaseless roaring
Speaks a voice, my heart restoring,—
        " Thou art asleep,
        " Thou art at rest,
" Thou art becalmed in the western bay."

Signs of Summer days returning
    Pass and linger round the hill,
Bright like flame the whins are burning,
    Even April winds are still ;
Every slumb'rous pulse of ocean
Murmurs with a fond emotion,—
        " Thou art asleep,
        " Thou art at rest,
" Calm as the deep is thy slumb'ring will."

Ah! when yet the leaves are falling
   On the death-couch of the year,
When the winds in wrath are calling,
   And the waves are white with fear;
'Mid the wildest nights of Winter
Calm with this one thought shall enter,—
    "Thou art asleep,
    "Thou art at rest,
"Thou art asleep, thou dost not hear."

GROWING OLD.

How is it, life, that when thy springs are young
   We prize thee then so lightly, letting be
   All-golden flowers of opportunity,
From the fleet moments leaving all unwrung
Gifts which they thirst to give us? Ah! 'tis sung
   To many a harp how strange the mystery
   Of pleasurable sorrow when we see
Far in the past the joys to which we clung!
But hath not rather this the larger power
   To quicken life with memorable pains,—
When in the strength of calmer manhood's hour
   The fact of being all its width explains,—
When, born at last, we haste from flower to flower,
   Because we know how little time remains?

"VERBUM SAP."

TEACH, but be patient also ; hast thou seen,
    Drawn from the bottom of the midway sea,
A tiny fossil, which hath erstwhile been
    The stronghold of some sea-born atomy ?

And hast thou, idly gazing at its shape,
    Lived through the years till haply it might lie
Upon the summit of some chalky cape
    That seems an emblem of eternity ?

Live through them, then, and ask thyself if such
    A space of time is linked with aught so dead,
May not the soul claim million times as much
    Before its life is half-way perfected ?

UPHILL.

Uphill and toward the open, so walk I ;
   Uphill, to where the city 'neath its shroud
   Of toil-born smoke, like an undrifting cloud,
Forms on one side the landscape's boundary ;
While on the other endless fields of sky
   O'er-arch an endless ocean, sparsely ploughed
   By far, faint ships, whence winds, now low, now loud,
Through scented firwoods musically sigh.
Ah ! 'tis no light attraction that doth sway
   My footsteps thus to wander, thus to find
Some respite from the narrower walks of day ;
   Surely 'tis this,—the impulse of the mind
To turn from what is touched, and cleave its way
   To where new largeness ever lies behind.

THE POET SPEAKS.

He speaks,—but first
From his deep chest comes forth a storm of sighs,
As if the veil to burst
That shrouds his soul from this world's spies.

He speaks,—yet no ;
Not with such ease the oracle is born ;
The costly tear-drops flow
Down his cheek's furrows, deeply worn.

" Ah, when," saith he,
As to himself in answer, not to us,
" Shall God's vast mystery
Cease to perplex his children thus ?

" O for a word,
My God, to make thy healing message known,
Translating what I heard
That time I spake with Thee alone !

"Heard ye my sighs?
With million, million sighs more deep than mine
　　The whole earth lifts its eyes
　In search for aught to call divine.

"Saw ye my tears?
By these I know, but know not surely when,
　　That every midnight wears
　At last to morn.　Amen, amen!"

FAILURE.

Of all the piteous evils upon earth
   This often seems the greatest,—when to one
   Who with bright hopes life's action hath begun,
Valiant in fight, a conqueror by birth,
There comes defeat, not through defect of worth,
   Not from o'er-rating that he might have done,
   But through some weakness, palpable to none,—
Neglected armour or a faulty girth.
O when such chances, if indeed there be
   Those who o'erlook with not impartial eyes
The lists of life, who wait in hope to see
   Their champion grasp the splendours of the prize,
Methinks those watchers' bootless agony
   Would make a gloom midmost in Paradise.

FIRST LOSS.

They laid him in the orchard shade,
    My dear old dog that died,
And on the grass mound, newly made,
    I sit at eventide.

I feel a grief that grows intense :
    'Tis foolish so to be;
And yet I have a strong, strange sense
    Of something gone from me.

And now it lives I know not where,—
    Whether in sea or sky,
Or in the purple twilight air,
    Or yonder cloud piled high.

Or in the spark which slowly grows
    A planet overhead,
And drops a hope upon my woes
    Fine as a golden thread.

"THIS MAN CALLETH FOR ELIAS."

" Let be," they cried, " and let Elias come,
    Even if he will, and save him." So they said,
    Not knowing that each thorn-thrust round that head,
Each drop from hand or foot, each moment dumb
With heart-locked anguish, added to the sum
    Of joy that o'er the unheeding nations shed
    A light more rare than ever day-dawn spread
O'er far-off summits from its eastern home.
So still " let be " the world cries out for those
    Who on their self-sought Calvary fulfil
Acts of redemption, so their priceless woes
    Reap but the laugh of mockery, and still
Elias comes not ; yet more radiant grows
    The dawn of God's all-purifying will.

QUITE HAPPY.

I AM a queen, a queen, a queen,
    A queen for a whole long day!
My kingdom is this sunlit green,
    My crown this rosebud spray.

O who will drain with me the cup
    That overflows with glee?
Alone I cannot drink it up,
    And shall it wasted be?

O little cloud, come down and play
    With me this happy tide!
Why should'st thou float alone all day
    Above the brown hillside?

O little brook, thy bed forsake,
    And tell me all the tales
Thou sing'st alone by bank and brake
    Along the woodland vales.

QUITE HAPPY.

O murmuring dove, forsake thy nest
   That rocks against the sky!
Thy head upon my bosom rest,
   And thence contented fly.

For I have got a heart so light
   That should the whole world lay
Its woes upon that heart to-night
   'Twould melt them all away.

I am a queen, a queen, a queen,
   A queen for a whole long day;
And through the sweet, and o'er the green,
   Till eventide I stray.

PARTNERSHIP.

"Work in my vineyard, this shall be thy fee";—
   Not so, my lord, for if my heart dissent
   From what my hands perform, shall discontent
By such a guerdon compensated be?
And if, perchance, I labour willingly,
   What need of wages? In thy service spent
   My life would count each drop that slowly went
As so much wealth received direct from thee.
O if thou plant, and if thou look to drain
   One day the cup of newly vintaged joy,
   Let not for me the hireling's part destroy
My hope (I care not if the hope be vain)
   To sit with thee, what time thy feast is spread,
   And share, as guest, the wine I helped to tread.

REMINISCENCES.

I SEE them in the night, my child,
    I see them in the day;
A shadowy throng that moves along,
Silent sometimes, sometimes with song,
    The years long passed away.

I see them in the night, my child,
    And dark they seem by day;
While those at night are always bright,
And each one bears a flickering light
    That shines across my way.

What is their shape, you ask, my child?-
    In truth I cannot say;
At times they seem a hurrying stream
Of angels in an angel's dream,—
    An angel pure as they.

And what sometimes, you ask, my child?
    In truth I dare not say;
As countless hosts of threatening ghosts
That wave me from eternal coasts;—
    And then I kneel and pray.

REWARD IN DUE SEASON.

High seems the task of those, who, undismayed
   By threat of loss, or by the world's cold scorn,
   Uplift the standard of a fairer morn
Upon the earth's dark places; who upbraid
Sloth by clear action, making much afraid
   The tottering potentates who long have borne
   Rule over life, till their throne-steps were worn
With feet of crowds who, loathing, yet obeyed.
High seems their task and bright their crown; but thou,
   Who, watching still the ocean depths of mind,
See'st but in these the restless ebb and flow
   Of partial currents,—look not thou to find
In time thy recompense; enough to know
   That wider work is guerdon'd in its kind.

OLD BOGIE.

Rumble up and rumble down,
    All about the crazy house!
Shall a ghost not claim his own?
    Shall a goblin not carouse?

Red the sun went down last night,
    And the moon was clear and thin;
Marked I not her crescent bright
    Bending round the orb within?

Lo! to-night the west is dark,
    And the moon is quenched in cloud;
Dripping gusts across the park
    Every instant wax more loud.

Owls are silent; rats are fled,—
    In their chambers scared and still;
All night long the restless dead
    Hold their revelries at will.

OLD BOGIE.

Now the children in their beds
   Hear me moving on the stair,
Straightway hide their trembling heads,
   Folding little hands in prayer.

Now the maid whose heart was stout,
   In the garret shrieks to find,
As her candle flickers out,
   Something touching her behind.

Now before the smouldering fire,
   Where he dozes o'er his wine,
With an oath the red-faced squire
   Feels a breath and knows it mine.

Now along the gallery wall
   Suddenly the lightning flames,
Shows the portraits, one and all,
   Laughing loudly in their frames.

All within is wakeful dread,
   All without is stir and strain,
House and stable, barn and shed,
   Are not all in my domain?

Now to whirl the scattered stack
   Over hedge and road and field;
Now to close the gravelled track
   With the elm that would not yield.

Now, with doubled might and main,
  On the streaming roofs to fall,
Till the watch-dog howls again,—
  Snorts the cart-horse in his stall.

Rumble up and rumble down
  Till the morning rises late;
Shall a goblin not make known
  When he visits his estate?

ASSOCIATION.

Who that on wheels of iron much hath sped,
   And watched the fleeting landscape, nook by nook,
   Like scarce read leaves of an unvalued book,
Unfold itself before him, hath not said :—
" This shadowed field is alway visited
   By thoughts of some far off ; to some this brook
   Hath all the voice and all the searching look
Of friends with whom the days of childhood fled " ?
So hath the art which lives in moulded sound,
   Or that which deals enchantment to the eye,
Unnumbered sympathies which are not found
   Alike in separate spirits ; which defy
Restraint of law and all artistic bound,
   And live unknown to crowds who pass them by.

FAIRY LAND.

Underneath the azure bells
  Where the tiny beech-nuts fall,
There the sweet Titania dwells,—
  There doth hold her festival.

When the bee no longer flies,
  When the mouse is snugly curled,
And the red full moon doth rise
  Seeming larger than the world :—

Then by paths through tangled grass
  Which above their crests doth bend,
All her fairy knights do pass
  On her bidding to attend.

Shield and hauberk there are seen,
  Pluméd helm and pennoned lance ;
Moonbeams oft, with tell-tale sheen,
  On the golden breast-plate glance.

Oftentimes they pause and wait,
  Oftentimes they list around,
Lest the reaper, labouring late,
  Find them marching o'er his ground.

Treasures to their queen they bring—
   Trophied arms and proofs of skill;
Feathers from the hedgeling's wing—
   Gold-dust from the granite rill.

Lo! from every side they come,
   Pressing to her court betimes;
On the darkness floats a hum
   Fainter than in summer limes.

Yonder on the bank she sits,
   Glow-worms ranged on either hand;
Offer, knights, as well befits,
   Homage to your queen's command.

Till the light from eastern wolds
   On the dreaming earth doth fall,
Here the sweet Titania holds
   Stately court and festival.

PROCRASTINATION.

"Wait till to-morrow,"—'tis the sluggard's plea;
   The sluggard who by long disuse hath made
   Action more hateful than some charnel shade
Where crowned corruption holds sole sovereignty.
Wait till to-morrow;—yet this word may be
   To some, perchance, whose souls are all but laid
   In grief's despairing fetters, who upbraid
Far-standing death that will not set them free,—
This word not seldom may to such become
   The voice that bids them yet resign once more,
Once more and only once, to sleep the sum
   Of their distraction,—that, beside the door
Of joy which opes at morning, standeth dumb,—
   The well-pleased servant whose high task is o'er.

CHILD-DREAMS.

The fire is dying spark by spark
   From curtain, floor, and wall;
All things look strangely in the dark,
   And I look strange to all.

Now in each hushed and gloomy nook
   Methinks some creature lies;
I cannot tell—I dare not look,
   Lest I should see their eyes.

My bed is now a golden boat,
   And bears a golden sail,
And over golden seas we float
   Where never breathed a gale.

And now we climb a mountain-side,
   Now trace the chestnut lane;
Now over city roofs we glide,
   And now dip down again.

O is it you, my lost white cat,
   That wait to meet me here?
And have you really brought me that
   Which is to me most dear?—

My twin-born sister, tiny Jane,
   Who died before I knew?
And must she, must she go again,
   And is this dream untrue?

A gathering sound is in my ears
   Through which she fades away,
And scarcely have I time for tears,
   For lo! once more 'tis day!

SELF-KNOWLEDGE.

'Tis said, but falsely, oftentimes of one
    Who from the deadly imminent breach of fate
    Has proved his right to rank among the great,
'Tis said he scarce his victory had won
Except his thoughts, deep-gifted to outrun
    The envious present, all the imperial state
    Of coming honours had foreseen, the gate
Of Fame's clear temple shining like the sun
Across the smoke of battle. So 'tis said,
    But falsely ; for the souls that thinly climb
To earth's supremest places are not led
    By such desires ; they rather stand sublime
In knowledge of their greatness, and instead
    Of living, lo ! they *are*, and know not Time.

THE GROUND SWELL.

WHAT seek'st thou, restless soul,
    Here by the bleak sea-side?
What find'st thou in the roll
    Of this unquiet tide
That seems a charm to make thy dulness whole?

Above the lightless main
    The soundless evening droops;
In single drops of rain
    The gathered fog-bank stoops;
A chill breeze wakes, then quickly dies again.

From yonder dim gray floor
    A wall of green uprears;
Swiftly it rolls to shore,
    Its noise is in my ears;
The beach gleams white, then turns to brown once more.

What seek'st thou, restless heart,
    Here by the bleak sea-side?
What charm, what wizard art
    Hath this unquiet tide
To hold thee gazing till the tear-drops start?

THE GROUND SWELL.

O but the roar grows loud !
    There will be storm anon ;
A blast through yonder cloud
    Will call its legions on
To waste the cliffs that wear a front so proud.

O but my heart's dull swell
    Grows loud from deep to deep,
And gathering voices tell
    The eyes that fain would weep
How for the soul that tempest will be well.

COMPROMISE.

"No man can serve two masters"; yet how strange
   That all men must do that which no man can;
   That, not to lose life's too contracted span,
Or float like bubbles on the breast of change,
Two worlds must be considered,—one whose spread
   Finds ever-widening circles, while to scan
   Too close the other's ever-narrowing plan
Brings mole-like blindness. Yet might it be said
That he well serves a master mightier still
   Who, with his soul's clear windows opened wide
To catch all wisdom, daily bends his will
   To render life due justice, to divide
Pretence from truth, and, where it mocks his skill,
   With half a truth to rest well satisfied.

FORWARDS!

Upon this ridge we pause awhile,
   And watch the battle round us bend,
Here, breathless all from file to file,
   We wait the signal to descend.

And now we watch the foe retreat,
   And now behold a friend struck low,
As still through smoke beneath our feet
   We mark the tumult ebb and flow.

We know not when our turn may come,
   We know not what the end will be;
And to our hearts fly thoughts of home
   Like land-birds to the ships at sea.

   *   *   *   *   *

Ah me! is this the well-known gate
   That opens on the well-known lane,
Where children joy to linger late,
   And lovers part to meet again?

Ah me! is this the honoured face
    Of him whose whisper bade me go
And seek some other resting-place
    If once my eyes refused the foe?

And is the warning just and true
    That he who leaves not all behind,
But 'mid the conflict holds in view
    Some idol dearer to his mind

Than zeal to work his land renown,
    Unworthy is for this to wear
Upon his brow the warrior's crown,
    Or claim a mourning comrade's tear?

*   *   *   *   *

But hark! the trumpet loudly blown!
    And see! the leader's sword on high!
And from our throats a cheer is thrown
    Right upward to the answering sky.

As one we step, as one we will
    That should success be far away
Except the sun and moon stand still,
    Yet ours at last shall be the day!

WORK.

Work for the sake of work, or work to be
   The scaling-ladder to some loftier aim
   Than seems such work to furnish? Thus I came
To reason once, not seeking carelessly,
But with desire to make what I should see
   The fittest rule, all powerful to enflame
   Life with some splendid purpose, rendering tame
The mere bare fact of the reality
Of self-existence. Long thereto I wrought;
   And, circling foiled about Truth's central sun,
There stole one day this whisper through my
      thought :—
   "Why labour thus? Behold, the things are one;
He aims who works; and oft the end unsought
   Crowns with strange glory work for work's sake
      done."

STEWART'S SWORD.*

The sword that flashed 'mid cannon smoke,
    When, backward pressed with many a bruise,
The Empire legions turned and broke,
    From Tagus up to fair Toulouse;—

That sword a worthy scion bestowed
    In friendship on the chief whose band
Had snatched the victory Freedom owed,
    Ev'n from the hosts of Freedom's land.

He passed; and even yet the smile
    Of peace was fresh o'er southern plains,
When, by the many-winding Nile,
    His blood made rich the battle stains.

His life sank down; his fame unrolled
    Like stars through midnight's opening rift;
"Not mine," that chieftain cried, "to hold
    The regal warrior's regal gift!

* See Note.

STEWART'S SWORD.

"This sword, whose laurels, reaped in Spain,
   Are twined with myrtle from the soil
Where Hope, long absent, seeks again
   To make stones bread by chymic toil ;—

"This sword shall gleam where kindred tears
   Shall own its call to kindred ends ;
A trophy for the far-off years
   Where Peace and Honour move as friends!"

ON THE THRESHOLD.

LIKE one who standeth musing at the door
    Through which his bride hath lately taken her way
    Unto the couch which, ere the break of day,
Shall be the witness of that boundless store
Of joys which true love opens ; who, before
    His steps pass onward, bids his heart to stay
    Its eager pace, lest thither it convey
Some thought unfit to cross that sacred floor ;—
So stand we now at this new gate of time,
    With silent lips and heads bent down in prayer,
Lest aught of self should, like a tempter, climb
    Into the paradise which God makes fair ;
And drive us forth, lashed by the scourge of crime,
    To till that life whose fruits are called despair.

THE SHADOW OF LOVE.

Love went forth with the dawn, with the dawn of a
    godlike day ;
Love, the beloved of men, went forth on his godlike
    way ;
From the warm blue seas of the South to the wilds of
    the sunless land—
Love with life on his lips, and Love with a sword in
    his hand.

Love went forth with the dawn ; but with Love went
    ever and aye
A Shadow that gibed and mocked, a Shadow of black
    dismay ;
Love went forth with the dawn, but there followed,
    from land to land,
Lust with death on his lips, and Lust with gold in his
    hand.

THE SHADOW OF LOVE.

Love went forth with the dawn, as a sower sowing his grain,
And the white-walled cities of peace sprang up from the populous plain;
Love went forth, but Lust in his footsteps scattered the tares,
And the white-walled cities of peace were white-tombed cities of snares.

The fierce-browed Puritan cried from his home in the cold stern north,—
"Strike, in the name of Christ! Strike, brothers, and drive them forth!
Strike with a sword of fire, and shatter the rule of Lust!
E'en perish the lips of Love, if perish for this they must!"

But Christ and the Mother of Christ, the calm-browed Mother and Child,
Looked down on the Puritan's wrath, looked down with reproof that smiled;
"This wrath is not mine," He said, "nor mine the tares that have grown
Wherever the full-eared wheat in the morning-time was sown.

"And whose is the love that is pure? And whose is
  the lust that is grained
By never a single spark of a love that might shine
  unstained?
And whose is the hand that shall haste, and whose is
  the hand that hath power
To sever and sift in the field? Let them wait till the
  harvest hour.

"But mine are the lips of Love, and mine is the sword
  of pain,
Smiting asunder the soul that hath bartered its love
  for gain;
The sword that is bright with tears in the anguish of
  silence shed,—
The sword that awakes to life when the lust and the
  gold are dead."

A DIP INTO KEATS.

Singer of Latmos and the Grecian urn,
    Within thy pages, howsoever rude
    Their shelved apparel, dwells a multitude
Of shapes that on our bleak existence turn
Fresh lips and eyes, as if in sooth to learn
    By what hard fate, for what defect from good,
    Life labours from its forehead to exclude
That light for which all breathing creatures yearn.
To thee, from conflict with tyrannic powers,
    We turn, as to some fountain wide and rare,
Around whose marge the golden-fingered hours
    Creep with no sense of motion, while the air,
    Warm without sadness, trembles everywhere
To wings that brush imperishable flowers.

NIGHT AND DEATH.

Night, fold me to thy side!
Fades now the eventide,
Fades now the landscape wide,
   Cold, cold grows the plain!
Wet were the morning's feet,
Fierce, fierce the noontide heat,
Yet brought the evening sweet
   Peace once again.
Night, fold me to thy side,
Bring me gentle slumber.

Death, fold me to thy side,
At life's last eventide,
When life's last lingering pride
   Breaks, breaks at thy word!
Wild though the morning's light,
Fierce, fierce the noonday fight,
Yet comes there truce at night,
   Rest from the sword.
Death, fold me to thy side,
Bring me gentle slumber.

COMING CHANGE.

A TIME there was when mankind on the earth,
    Strong creatures of the moment, lived and bred
    In thoughtless beauty, compassed not by dread
Of aught beyond the hour. Then came the birth
Of creeds that linked with plenty or with dearth
    Supremer judgments, till all freedom fled,
    And joy scarce dared bind garlands round its head,
Lest they should mar the penitential worth
Of daily mutilation. So things fared—
    Joy swallowed up by hopeless dreads of sin—
Till now, perchance, some whisper may be heard
    Bidding mankind a richer life begin,—
Bidding them link, in union long prepared,
    Knowledge with happiness, and dwell therein.

A CHRISTMAS GREETING.

No frosty foliage dims the pane,
    No snowdrifts clog the silent ways,
No feathery flake, no star-traced Wain,
    Blesses the roof or cheers the gaze.

The night is hushed ; the winds are warm ;
    The mists trail past from star to star,
With low-breathed mutterings of the storm
    Like sounds of battle heard from far.

So changed the sky ; yet not for them
    Are changed the thoughts to memory dear,
Who in the shrine of Bethlehem
    Salute with peace the parting year.

Not changed for them the pause from strife,
    Not changed the yearning to forgive ;
Nor changed the hope to win from life
    Some gracious crown for all that live.

Not changed the clasp that mutely speaks
   Of conflicts in Time's distant field ;
Not changed the tournament that breaks
   Love's lance on honour's spotless shield.

Not changed the spell that kinship throws
   O'er hearts that childhood's faith re-learn,
And, circled, seem to sit with those
   Whom sea or land no more return.

Break, gently break, O day that seems
   To desert wanderers not too wise,
A star that guides, by fitful gleams,
   To where the world's salvation lies.

Break, break in mist, or break in flame !
   And bring, to crown this peerless morn,
Such songs as to the shepherds came
   That very tide when Christ was born.

LIGHT IN DARKNESS.

With rush of wheel and click of pattering hoof
   The dull December morning wakes, and spares
   Some dim brown twilight to the leafless squares,
While dingy smoke-wreaths creep from roof to roof.
Man goeth forth ; each footfall seems a proof
   With what incessant labour he repairs
   The walls that front a rising tide of cares
In homes from which all brightness holds aloof.
Gloom reigns without, the sense of strife within ;
   Yet through the gloom streams down a golden ray
To light the roof where even now begin
   Soft trembling pulses of a life which they,
To whom it comes, shall find a charm to win
   Peace from the perils of the world's highway.

THE HOPE THAT IS IN US.

Not for the gift of endless years,
    Not for the sake of cleansing fires,
Nor hope to grasp, through grief and tears,
    The crown of unfulfilled desires :—

Not, not for this the soul implores
    To feel, when life's last light is waning,
The sense of self on dawning shores,
    And memory still its strength retaining.

Not, not for this ; but O, most strong
    The wish in juster worlds to waken,
And learn through years to heal each wrong
    Once wrought through facts or aims mistaken.

To find in some approaching shade
    Some life which once we sorely wounded,
To see how deep the gash we made
    With thoughts unjust, with scorn unfounded.

And as, 'mid light that all unstrips,
　　Each as himself beholds the other,
To murmur, with repentant lips,—
　　" Alas ! I erred ; forgive me, brother ! "

A. C. SWINBURNE.

Ah me! thy world is not a world like ours,
   High priest of one great love and many woes,
   Whose voice is like the Autumn wind that blows
O'er wasted fields and wreck of Summer bowers.
Ah me! if e'er the spring-time lost its flowers,
   If e'er July his rapturous noontide glows,
   If light turned dark, or Joy forgot to close
Her temple gates against the avenging Hours ;—
Yet should my steps to thy strange warbling move
   Through golden climes, through fields at all times fair
With purple bloom and many a haunted grove ;
   Or, without heed enticèd on to where
   The music seemed to centre, find thee there,
With cypress crowned amid the walks of love.

   1868.

THE LAST WALTZ.

The lights die down ; a touch of dawn
   Gleams faintly through the draperied pane ;
At last breathes forth, with notes long drawn,
   The final waltz's opening strain.

The theme thrills on—the floor is free ;
   Scarce half-a-dozen couples now
Float round where lately tossed a sea
   Of gems that flashed on beauty's brow.

The hands that clasp, the lips that smile,
   Ere night may clasp and smile once more,
And memories of the dance beguile
   Fair conclaves of the musked boudoir.

So they ; but what, my love, to us
   Imports this faint and pleading air,
Whose hearts are celebrating thus
   The vigil of a life's despair ?

To-night the love we may not own
  Enfolds us with its icy veil;
To-morrow finds us each alone,
  Beyond the bounds of touch or hail.

In death the wrecked, in sleep the tired
  May find the welcome end of care,
But even death is scarce desired
  By hearts that must not break, but bear.

Ah me! 'tis come, that morn of sighs!
  No more delayed the final smart!
Slow, slow, the music sinks and dies;
  With one long lingering clasp we part.

With one long lingering clasp—no more;
  Yet in our souls that dying strain
Will sob for ever on the shore
  That bounds the inexorable main.

"NIHIL FECI; AMAVI TANTÚM."

"I have done nothing; I have only loved";—
   And was not that, O suffering heart, enough?
   "Nothing" and "only"; are we of such stuff
That by thy silent tragedy unmoved
We tread with joy the world's ways, which have proved
   To thee too bleak with bitterness, too rough
   For life's endurance? Breathes there no rebuff
From thy sad station? Lightly have we roved,
Like bees that court the sunshine, draining still
   Their little cups of gladness, while each flower
Laughs in their faces, heeding not, until—
   Symbol of grief's all-penetrating power—
Some rose-crowned crucifix upon the hill
   Spreads silence through the noontide's murmuring hour.

THE VIOLIN'S STORY.

A welcome warmth my being filled,
   Born from her bosom's charm,
While all the soul of music thrilled
   Adown her dimpled arm.

I caught the sweetness of her lips ;
   I heard, I felt, her sigh ;
And marked the crystal tear's eclipse
   That gently dimmed her eye,

Her heart was full ; she could not speak
   The love she'd fain declare ;
But I was strong where she was weak,
   And boldly spake for her.

And as her touch of subtle art
   Sped o'er my trembling strings,
I told the burden of her heart
   And gave her secret wings.

Ah! great the power of woven sound
   To touch the heart's abyss!
For love that night his Eden found—
   A whisper and a kiss!

IN SOUNDINGS.

LIKE to a sea whose soundings show decrease
   Life stretches forward to the nearing shore
   Where ends this voyage.　Even now the roar
Of breakers sobs around us ; without cease
We drift and drift, 'mid calm that is not peace
   Nor expectation hope.　The labouring oar
   Lies idle, while we wearily explore
The gloom that wraps us.　Fain would we release,
Like those in Adria tost, all reckoning gone,
   Some anchor that might hold us till the day
Reveals what lies before us—whether won
   The haven of our search, or if the way
Through weary waters leaves us wrecked, alone,
   In desert islets of oblivion's sway.

A KISS FOR THE DEALER.

Ace, two, three, four,—a lucky trick!
    Ah, what, my girl!—your cheek grows paler?
You know the jest, or not so quick
    The blood would seek its fluttering jailer.

The dealer claims a kiss, and you—
    You dealt the cards which now we're playing,
And thus the cards take vengeance due,
    Perchance, for some inept betraying.

There's no one here; your cousin Meg,
    Behind her cards demurely smiling,
Would not refuse should any beg
    The forfeit won by such beguiling.

And Dick, your partner yet to be,
    Is waiting with serene diversion
To learn if aught of jealousy
    You look for as your life's reversion.

A KISS FOR THE DEALER.

There !—thus upon your dainty cheek
    I press the forfeit, nothing doubting
That if your lips would only speak
    They'd speak in thanks too grave for pouting.

For something in your heart can tell
    How true the faith of worship's donors
Who like to see a game go well,
    Though not for them the tricks and honours.

THE LIZARD LIGHTS.

TWIN lights, that meet the wanderer's gladdening gaze
   As through vexed Biscay's surges he returns,
   Seeking the port for which his spirit yearns,
With kind remembrances of far-off days ;
Even as the victor binds his brow with bays,
   So nightly round your lantern, where it burns,
   Twine thoughts more sacred than the votive urns
Recording rescue from those watery ways
Well-known of Palinurus.   Like a hand
   Waved from the shore in welcome, so your glow
Mounts skywards o'er the reaches of the land,
   Through fog-wreaths piercing, o'er the perilous flow
Of shoal-locked tides proclaiming its command,
   Steadfast as hope, and bright as homes we know.

A RAILWAY NOTE.

A STRAIGHT white ribbon lies the track
   Across the brown Karroo,
And looking forward, looking back,
   My love flies straight to you.

The earth lies broad and vast and still
   Beneath the dome of blue ;
Even so my heart and soul and will
   Lie hushed in love for you.

A STRAND STUDY.

MIDNIGHT well past, the world just sauntering home;
   The river silent; few the lighted panes;
   Stars overhead, while through the echoing lanes
Cool breaths from Surrey pastures faintly roam;
Yet sentried figures loiter in the gloom,
   Angling with smiles for scant and dubious gains,
   Dreading to face, through what of night remains,
Memories of youth and threatenings from the tomb.
"Because no man hath hired us." God, great God!
   Man in thy image, woman in her own,—
Earth's blossom of perfect beauty undertrod
   By that which sits in reason's loftiest throne!
And yet no prophet preaches of the rod
   Upraised in wrath for nature thus o'erthrown.

IN ARCADIA.

She came to my door in a kirtle of satin,
  With love-knots and roses to crown her array;
Her voice like the bird's that upsoars in the matin,
  Her breath like the incense that comes with the hay.
She came to my door when, 'twixt sleeping and waking,
In cold dreams of sadness and languor I lay;—
    "My darling, I love you!
    My darling, I love you!
My darling, I love you this sweet morn of May!"

I rose from my couch 'mid a tumult of blisses,
  And stretched forth my arms as the gloom dropped away;
Our lips mutely met in the sweetest of kisses,
  Our hearts throbbed together like wild birds at play.
No word could we speak, but the silence was making
Such music as star-beams and angels obey;—
    "My darling, I love you!
    My darling, I love you!
My darling, I love you this sweet morn of May!"

O far was all thought that could kindle our blushes—
  The heart's true embraces are clear as the day ;
Our love thrilled us through like the glory that flushes
  The hills of the East when the night swims away.
Yet hope sees a dawn when, from sweet dreams awaking,
  A soft pillowed whisper beside me shall say ;—
      " My darling, I love you !
      My darling, I love you ;
My darling, I love you this sweet morn of May ! "

ECCE HOMO!

ROBED in imperial purple, crowned with thorn,
   Behold the Man ! the being whose regal power
   Westward from Eden, since the anointing hour,
Hath grown from twilight to triumphant morn.
Thus robed, thus crowned ; but O ! how deeply torn
   The conquering brow ! How tragical the dower
   Of blood down-dropping in perpetual shower
On fields rough-ploughed in anguish for the corn
Of peace and fair contentment ! Wert not thou,
   O Man, condemned to labour for thy bread
Wrestling with thorns, in weary sweat of brow ?
   And lo ! those thorns grow luminous to shed
Bright benediction on the world that now
   Bears up the throne through pain inherited !

HER PROGRESS.

Dainties in the windows,—
  Watches, gowns, and rings;
Kitty, as she passes,
  Gives her fancy wings.

Wherefore should she labour
  Till her hands are brown,—
Half-a-dozen children
  Clinging to her gown?

Life *could* be so happy;
  Life *may* be so long;
All the world loves pleasure;
  Can it then be wrong?

Hers are youth and beauty;
  Men are seldom wise;
In the harlot's lottery
  She may draw the prize.

In the harlot's lottery,
  Spite its million blanks,
Some have won promotion
  Even from the ranks.

Wealth the mess of pottage,—
    Chastity the price;
Rose-trees and a cottage,—
    Just a little vice.

So the ticket's taken;
    So the game's begun;
Captured, foolish Kitty
    Captivating one.

Lazy, dainty Kitty,
    In her bird-cage life,
Strives to think with pity
    Of the toiling wife.

Then her lord grows weary;
    Indolence is sweet;
Kitty fain must worship
    Venus of the Street.

Sadder still she finds it,
    Noting day by day
How her dainty freshness
    Wears itself away

Underneath the gaslights,
    In the midnight rain;
Once she knew life's pleasure;
    Now she knows its pain.

Every brightness leaves her ;
   Soon the last leaves fall ;
God alone receives her,
   Understanding all.

A QUESTION.

What sayest thou, poet? Speak, for thou hast been
   With Israel's prophet in the echoing cave
   Of Horeb, where the thunder, wave on wave,
Rolled round thee like a flood that rolls between
The mainland and some rock whose crest of green
   Seems life's last foothold to the wretch whose grave
   Begins to rise around him,—speak, and save,
Where thou dost reap, some hope for us that glean!
Is this the boundary and the utmost end
   Of life reviving from the life that dies,
And doth the sun which we have seen descend
   Return no more to gladden yearning eyes?
Or is the darkness lingering but to lend
   Wealth to new dawns that wait in Orient skies?

EXPERIENCE.

Better too much life, surely, than too little,
   Better the tangled forest than the sand ;
Better to build with glass, and find it brittle,
   To lean on reeds until they pierce the hand.

Better,—for thus the spirit, slowly learning
   What things are false, at last perceives the true ;
Until, like some faint prodigal returning,
   It gladly grasps its Father's hand anew.

NOTES.

A Song of Peace.—In October, 1881, much anxiety was felt in South Africa as to the action of the Transvaal Volksraad (or Parliament) in respect of the Pretoria Convention, to several of the conditions of which the members of the Raad strongly objected. Any refusal to ratify the Convention would have been the signal for a renewal of hostilities, with probably most lamentable results for the whole country. Just about the time when the telegram announcing the ratification arrived in Pietermaritzburg, the weather was threatening, and a slight hailstorm occurred. With the promulgation of the news the weather cleared completely. The coincidence was noticed by a good many persons at the time.

Stewart's Sword.—After the conclusion of peace between Great Britain and the Transvaal burghers, in 1881, Sir Herbert (then Colonel) Stewart presented General P. J. Joubert, one of the Transvaal Triumvirate, with a sword which had been used by an ancestor in the Peninsular War. When Sir Herbert Stewart died in the effort to relieve Khartoum, General Joubert, who had highly appreciated such a token of regard, returned the sword to Sir Herbert Stewart's family, with a very graceful letter.

www.ingramcontent.com/pod-product-compliance
Lightning Source LLC
Chambersburg PA
CBHW021813230426
43669CB00008B/736